Random Walks in Solitude

Glimpses of Religion and Spirituality Through the Eyes of Modern Science

Anil Vishnu Moharir Ph. D.

With Foreword By
Dr. Vijay Pandurang Bhatkar
Ph. D., F. N. I., Padma Bhushan

ZORBA BOOKS

Published by Zorba Books, July 2024
Website: www.zorbabooks.com
Email: info@zorbabooks.com
Author Name: Anil Vishnu Moharir Ph. D.
Copyright ©: Anil Vishnu Moharir Ph. D.

Title: Random Walks in Solitude

Printbook ISBN: 978-93-5896-022-8
Ebook ISBN: 978-93-5896-775-3

Zorba Books Pvt. Ltd. (opc)
Sushant Arcade,
Next to Courtyard Marriot,
Sushant Lok 1, Gurgaon – 122009, India

Printed by Manipal Technologies Limited
A1 & A2 Shivalli Industrial Area Manipal Udupi, Karnataka – 57610

DEDICATED TO

Mrs. Sulochana Anil Moharir

(Nee Miss Sulochana Balkrishna Thakar)

Contents

Foreword

Dr. Vijay Pandurang Bhatkar
Ph. D. (IIT-Delhi), F. N. I., Padma Bhushan
Renowned Computer Scientist known for developing
India's Indigenous Super Computer PARAM 8000.
Former Chancellor, Nalanda International University,
Currently Chief Mentor-Multiversity Private Limited, Pune,
Maharashtra

The universe came into existence some 13.7 billion years ago and consists of only matter and energy, their interactions and manifestations of various kinds. The proverbial 'Big-Bang' from which it manifested has been studied and described in religious and scientific literature since time immemorial. The oldest scriptures that described its formation are the 'Vedas' from Bharat about 10,000 years ago and long after the intelligent human evolved with ability, inherent curiosity and capacity to comprehend the magnitude of dimensions involved and analytically correlate his own position in relation to universal creation. The ancient 'Rishis' discovered the natural laws that govern the universal material creation, sustenance, destruction and recycling. They recreated the sequence of biological and human evolution which has been described as the *'Dasha Avatars' (ten incarnations)* of the proverbial deity *'Vishnu'* from whom all the creation came into being. The author, Dr. Anil Vishnu Moharir, describes *'Vishnu'* to be a continuum of universal electric potential energy.

Scientists, identify four natural forces namely; Weak interaction, Strong interaction, Electromagnetism and Gravitation that govern the universal creation. Of these, the similar Weak and Strong interactions differ only in their range of operation. That leaves only three forces, which are primarily responsible for creation, sustenance and destruction of the universe. And amazingly, the 'Rishis' conceptualized this in the creation of a symbolical deity called –*The 'Dattatreya'*, a composite of three deities *'Brahma'* the creator, *'Vishnu'* the sustainer and *'Shiva'* the destroyer. The universe is a self-generating, self-sustaining and self-destroying phenomena, under control of the four forces of nature in a cycle. And human beings, have no option but to survive within the narrow limits of conditions provided to it by the nature. We cannot cross those limits and need to perform all our activities, procreation, adventure and explorations to satisfy our curiosity, by staying within those limits, strictly according to the natural laws. The 'duty-bound' strategies for our survival, have been compiled in the most profound scientific treatises the '*Vedas*'. The '*Vedic Sanatan Dharma*' as strategies for survival, irrespective of cast, creed, colour of skin, geographical location, nationality, personal bias or belief in any religious faith, was summarized in the 'Yog Sutra' by Sage Patanjali. The '*Vedas*' represent the pinnacles of intellectual, spiritual, scientific and analytical excellence of human mind. No surprise, seeds of everything that is being newly discovered in mathematics and science from the west, can be found and linked to discoveries mentioned in the *Vedas*'. For example, identical descriptions on the concept of 'Atom' and the 'Laws of Motion', attributed today to Sir Isaac Newton, can be found in the books written by '*Rishi*' Kanad, who lived before 300 CE. Observing, understanding and reasoning the physical world, with our mental faculty is certainly not disconnected from the eternal laws of the universe, and require a spiritual bent of mind called the '*Adhyatma*'.

Thousands of books and articles have been written explaining the effects of natural forces and their interactions with human body, mind, physiology, psychology and behavior for healthful survival under dynamically changing fluxes of energy from terrestrial, atmospheric, solar, planetary, galactic and cosmic sources. A bulk of these writings repeatedly discuss terminologies for the concepts, processes and effects as used by the ancient '*Rishis*' in Sanskrit and Prakrut languages. The demand of the hour being that our scientists in the twenty first century, must decode and identify all ancient terminologies in terms of their equivalent or closely synonymous modern scientific terminologies, so that they are automatically revalidated and easily understood by the young generation. This may generate, motivation, urge, interest, and perhaps invoke a sense of national pride in their minds to return back to the Vedic philosophy.

I have pleasure to see the efforts put in by Dr. Anil Vishnu Moharir, who is a trained physicist with vast experience of research in biology and agriculture to write very comprehensive, multidisciplinary articles explaining our ancient concepts from modern scientific point of view. He has not only described the importance but also their continued relevance, despite tremendous developments in science, technology and very high resolution instrumentation for quantification of physical concepts. In this book, Dr. Moharir has dealt with some of the most profound, subjectively controversial and scientifically most enigmatic subjects like spirituality, GOD, new world religion, science of *samadhi*, the proverbial *'Samudra Manthan'*, *'Prana'*, universal consciousness, *'Karma' and the Law of Karma'* and their inter-relationships for human survival on Earth. I am aware, whatever he has attempted to describe and synthesize in these articles, are not the last words. Several modifications, revisions, research and inputs may be required from the enlightened readers. Anticipating such possibilities, Dr. Moharir has at least taken the first step in this direction. It requires tremendous courage, self-confidence, convictions, multidisciplinary training, study and long hours in meditation and thinking to write something radically different, unconventional of this kind with logic and reason. The book offers a fresh look on all these ancient concepts and is exemplary as a practical guide on- 'How to think in an innovative way on any subject under investigation'.

I congratulate Dr. Anil Vishnu Moharir for publishing this book. Like a honey bee, randomly collecting nectar from flowers, the title of his book also reflects, the vast canvas of knowledge he has collected and logically linked together. Only a gifted individual can do it. I strongly recommend this book to all students in our universities and colleges. They would learn much more beyond their class room teachings from this book.

– Dr, Vijay Pandurang Bhatkar
Pune
Maharashtra

Preface

Ever since my childhood, I have always been drawn curious towards science and the 'Sanatan Vedic' Philosophy. My grandmother Late Shrimati Lakshmibai Baliram Moharir was a store-house of eloquent stories from the Ramayana, Mahabrarat, Upanishad and Bhagwat Puran, besides being an excellent story teller. And she had barely studied in any school in her childhood. My inquisitive mind always searched for scientific relevance and physical truth in those fanciful narration of stories by my grandmother. To, many of my questions on these stories and their characters, my grandmother was not comfortable, but she always managed to go ahead with at least some justification. Those questions remained into my sub-conscious mind all through my life. The habit of being inquisitive since childhood, helped me later in pursuing my career as a student of physics and as a scientific researcher in contributing original and innovative research papers in international research journals. Destiny, if there is anything like that, provided me with opportunity to work in the National Institute devoted to research in agriculture. As a trained postgraduate in physics, I had neither knowledge nor education in biology and agriculture. But knowing the fact, that the entire universe consists of nothing but only energy- matter interactions, and every material thing in the universe is made only of atoms, I soon picked up and took my roots into the unknown discipline and made my career in agricultural research.

My practical experience as a transmission electron microscope specialist, brought me face to face with biological units of life called the cells, their structure and compositions, interactions with environment and under attack by the parasites and pests of various kinds. I began to visualize, imagine, comprehend and correlate the amazingly complex energy-matter continuum that exists within the dimensional limits of human knowledge from 10^{-14} to 10^{30} cm, i.e. from the micro to the macro dimensions. I began to foster connections and linkages between apparently un-connected but amazingly inter-connected dimensions and disciplines.

Writing popular scientific articles in local and national magazines has been a passion with me since my school days and I pursued it during my university and service years also. After retirement from service, I have tried to devote as much time as possible and contribute something new, rather than keep writing on scientific subjects with the same routine arguments, logic and descriptions, repeatedly inherited by our society since time immemorial. The present book under the title- 'Random Walks in Solitude: Glimpses of Religion and Spirituality through the Eyes of Modern Science' is a collection of some of the most thought provoking articles published in diverse periodicals since 2006 AD, under one cover. And the topics include some of the most complex and enigmatic subjects such as 'Concept of *Prana*', 'Universal Consciousness', 'Scientific basis of *Samudra Manthan* the Proverbial Churning of Cosmic Ocean', '*Lord Dattatreya*', '*Ardha-Nari-Nateshwara*' and 'Science behind *'Yogic Samadhi'*. While doing so, I do not claim that my interpretations on some of these ancient enigmatic concepts are exactly true, but in the absence of any serious attempt by anyone so far, they feel refreshing and I have at least attempted to re-validate them on scientific logic and reasons. Otherwise we were just holding them dear to our hearts for thousands of years as fanciful stories. They were conceived and described then, by our ancient philosopher 'Rishis' in completely native terminologies and language and since then, have remained a part of our psyche in our life. Today, as professional scientists, we need to look to these enigmatic concepts afresh from modern scientific perspective, identify and correlate those concepts with current scientifically analogous terminologies, without losing their original perceptive concept and meaning, they conveyed to our minds. In this respect, my logical scientific interpretations of the concepts of 'Soul', 'Rebirth', 'Work' and the 'Law of Karma', published five years ago in the form of a book, have received considerable international attention and appreciation in the form of being adjudged as the 'Best Selling Title' in May 2024, even five years after it was first published. I therefore, feel encouraged to continue my pursuit in this direction and there is so much to do in this area of work. These attempts may provide a sense of 'National Pride' to our young generation, who are almost lost in the western educational curriculum that we unfortunately retained, even after independence. Besides, such articles, carry the necessary potential for stimulating and arousing curiosity towards *'Sanatan Vedic Philosophy'*. I hope, my current book would be welcomed by the enlightened readers and find it not only interesting but feel compelled to recommend and even present a copy of the same to the young members in their families for encouragement. *'Sanatan Vedic'* philosophy is a true scientific treatise, perennially relevant for all times to come and therefore irrespective of any cast, creed, religious faith, beliefs, colour of skin, location on earth and nationalities. '*Sanatan* Vedic Philosophy and Dharma' indeed, constitute the cardinal scientific truth for healthy survival, under all kinds of environmental, physical, physiological and psychological conditions on Earth.

All the articles are sequentially independent and readers may begin to read from any one of their interest. In view of this, some repetitions may be observed in articles, on subjects which are very closely related. And I have intentionally left them so, to save my readers from referring back each time for connecting links. Similarly, references given at the end of each article have been retained so, instead of consolidating them at the end of the book.

Unless mentioned specifically, all the befitting figures, illustrations and photographs, I have used for explanation of my view point in the articles included in this compilation, have been downloaded from the 'Pinterest'website' under their policy of allowing free download for public education.

My earlier compilation under nearly identical title containing 13 individual articles was published in 2013. In doing so, my wife Mrs. Sulochana Anil Moharir has provided me enough leisure to be sitting and writing at my work table. But for her personal sacrifice and legitimate demand on my time for herself, this would have been almost impossible. For over fifty two years of our togetherness, she has been tolerating my whimsical passion for writing, possibly answering or interpreting same questions that I had been seeking answers to, since childhood without satisfaction. I therefore dedicate this compendium to Mrs. Sulochana Anil Moharir as my humble tribute with gratitude for everything she has done for me and my life. I am equally grateful to my loving daughter Prachi Moharir, for her constant encouragement and giving valuable feedback, comments and suggestions after reading all my article, despite her health issues and extremely busy work schedule from England. Her knowledge of human psychology and management skills were especially advantageous to me in effectively editing all these articles.

I am fortunate, that Padma-Bhushan Dr. Vijay Pandurang Bhatkar, FNI, with a remarkable bearing in both modern science and spirituality should have agreed to my request to write the foreword to this compilation. Besides, his invaluable contribution in indigenously developing Super-Computer PARAM 8000 and other advanced versions, making our country self-reliant for innumerable applications in national programs on planning, administration and developmental activities. Dr. Bhatkar is also known for studies and knowledge in the realm of 'Sanatan Vedic Philosophy' and Spirituality. His celebrated book on the scientific thoughts of Shri Gulabrao Maharaj, a well-known philosopher saint from Maharashtra and scientific interpretation of 'Bhagwad Gita' are the most sought after books in the books market. There could not have been a better person for me than Respected Dr. Vijay Pandurang Bhatkar to write the foreword for a compilation of articles that describe subjects from the domain of religion and spiritualty from purely modern scientific point of view. I am sincerely grateful to him for doing me this honour.

– Anil Vishnu Moharir
M. Sc. Physics, Ph. D. IIT-Delhi
Retd. Professor and Head
Division of Agricultural Physics
Indian Agricultural Research Institute
New Delhi

Pune, Maharashtra
July 17, 2024 Corresponding to
Ashadh Shuddha 11 (AShadhi Ekadashi)
Shak Samvat 1946.

CHAPTER – 1

Science Spirituality and GOD: An Attempted Synthesis

Dimensions of human knowledge and inter-play of matter and energy in the universe

Each tiny sparkling dot in the 'Milky Way' seen in the night sky is in fact a galaxy (group) consisting of 1 million individual stars stretching across from its one end to the other by a distance of hundred or thousand light years. This means light at its speed of One lakh Eighty Six Thousand Miles per second (1,86,000 miles/second OR 3×10^{10} m/second) will take thousand years to go from one end of the tiny dot to its other end. And there are one million such galaxies in one universe and millions of such universe still beyond. The known portion of the Universe observed so far, through the best of telescopic instruments extends for approximately 10^{10} light years, or 10^{28} cm. The smallest known distance from the knowledge of atomic and Elementary particle physics is 10^{-14} cm. A comparison of the smallest to the greatest distances yields the staggering number 10^{42} cm.

The smallest distance of 10^{-14} cm is traversed by light at its speed in 10^{-24} seconds. This is then the smallest time interval and it lies far beyond the limits of all known methods of time measurements. The greatest time interval we know is the "lifetime of the universe' since its creation from the moment the proverbial 'Big Bang' estimated to have occurred 10,000 million and 30,000 million years or 10^{18} seconds ago. Again, a comparison of the smallest and greatest time intervals yields a value of 10^{42}. Incidentally, this coincidence of magnitude of time and distance intervals is not by chance but there seems to be some secret of creation hidden behind this correspondence in tune with the mystery of the constancy of the several universal physical constants. There is no explanation for why these constants are there as they are and we have no choice but to accept them as "given"- imprinted on the universe like the maker's trade-mark at the moment of cosmic creation and fixed forever. As a scientist, we have therefore no option but to believe that both the macro- and micro- universe is governed by some absolutely dependable, universally invariable, mathematical laws of unknown origin, inter-connected, related or regulated by the universal physical constants. And the very fact that the physical laws just exist without a valid logical reason is scientifically anti-rational according to Paul Davis.

As we know, the remotest sections of the universe are receding from us at the velocities close to that of light. Electromagnetic energy, predominantly in the form of light connects the two extreme infinities i.e. the infinity of vastness and infinity of minuteness and provides information about the micro and distant cosmic worlds. These are the dimensions of human knowledge. There is only matter and energy that fills this vast expanse of the universe and their interplay in between creates material world of various kinds, beautifully summarized by Einstein's theory of relativity and his famous equation ($E = m.C^2$), where E stands for energy, m for mass of the matter and C for the velocity / of light). The fundamental physical constants, in contradiction to the unity of nature are characterized for the sake of convenience into two groups. The first one includes the type of constants used to describe the macro-world, whereas the constants of the second group characterize the behavior of the smallest microphysical particles, which cannot be observed directly. Since any macro-object is nothing else but a collection of a huge number of atoms, the two worlds i.e. the micro and the macro must necessarily be interrelated, **Figure-1**.

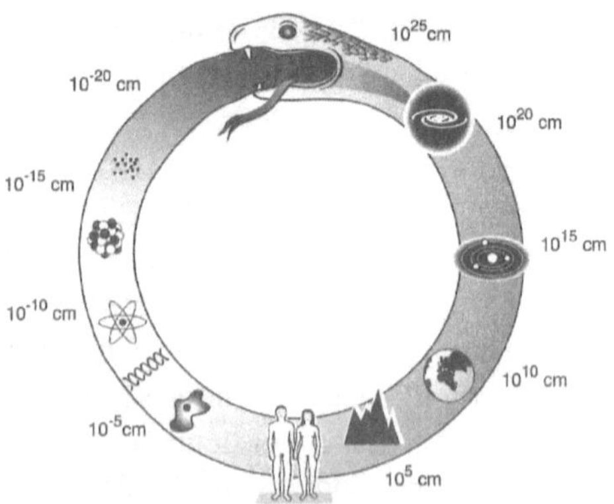

nuclei and atoms (left) and the cosmos (right). *(Reproduced with kind permission)*

Figure 1. The *Ouraborus*. There are links between the microworld of particles, *from Sir Martin Rees from 'Just Six Numbers by Martin Rees, Phoenix, 1999.*

Finding such connections or links is one of the challenging problems of current physics and until this is done, the edifice of physics will not be completed. Furthermore, the values of the constants are not obtained theoretically but have to be measured experimentally. Therefore, in probing the universe, man actually probes his own brain and nature of his boldest and craziest theories are determined by his way of thinking. They are mirrors that reflect our capability for knowledge, and Man is indeed born for knowledge and he shall never stop in seeking his own reality, purpose and place in the scheme of universal creation. It is this pursuit with logic and reason based on observed facts; man has invented various branches of sciences to understand the manifestation of nature and their sociological interactions. Therefore, a physicist who concerns himself with any event that takes place at various levels in between the limits of infinities is called by various names such as a cosmologist, Helios-physicist, astrophysicist, cosmic ray physicist, atmospheric physicist, meteorologist, environmental physicist, geologist, soil-physicist, mineralogist, metallurgist, solid state physicist, nuclear physicist, elementary particle physicist, meta-physicist, bio-physicist, molecular biophysicist and so on. However, this classification was and is purely arbitrary and leads only to misconceptions and disastrous conditioning of human mind, because knowledge is an inter-linked continuum without discreet boundaries. Every specialist from all branches of sciences referred above, in fact, searches and re-searches only an inter-play of matter and energy from his own perception.

Man, on the face of the earth, lives in a world of material things of infinitely diverse kind, created, sustained and recycled under the influence of four types of primary forces of nature recognized by physicists as; weak interaction, strong interaction, electromagnetic and gravitation. A mysterious super attractive (not the kind of gravity) 'fifth force' originating at the interface of the universe has also been contemplated. This 'fifth force' is believed to differ from gravitation in that it is exerted on the matter itself and not on the mass of matter as gravitation does. The proposed Large Hadron Collision Experiment at the CERN, Geneva is a step further in our understanding the nature of material creation in the universe and its ultimate constitution. However, the most baffling and complex being our 'consciousness', its origin, nature, characteristics, manifestation and process of recycling. Scientists are yet to recognize 'consciousness' as a natural force in line with the other four forces already known. The oldest known scientific literature and philosophy in the world –the 'Vedas' and the 'Upanishads' clearly indicate that the material creation of the universe took place about 15 billion years ago starting from the primordially dispersed high density magnetic field to electric field; from electric field to electromagnetic field; from electromagnetic field to gaseous and liquid state matter and from gaseous and liquid state to solid state in the same chronological order. What does not fit into this sequence of creation is the destructive universal gravitational field, independent of all other forces and which pervades all through the material creation. Unlike electric and magnetic forces, gravitation is only an attractive type of force. The electric charge being the starting point for the creation of molecules and visible matter, of various kinds and structures. This is in perfect agreement with modern concepts of theoretical chemistry based on the exchange / share of electron charge between invisible atoms of different kind leading to formation of structures. Obviously therefore, if there is a common origin for all these eventful sequence in creation, they should be able to be explained by a common physical theory and therefore the search for such theory of everything is on. One commentator on an article published in 'The Scientist.com' has rightly put it in appropriate spirit- "The theory of unification requires an insanely broad mind-not necessarily in terms of detailed comprehension, but rather endowed with infinite innocence and curiosity". No wonder, why Albert Einstein should have spent last four decades of his life in attempt to search for a theory of nature in which all laws of matter and energy would be unified. The ultimate purpose of human existence being to understand how the events in this world of material things are interlinked for the creation and survival of plant, animal, insect, microbes and humankinds. It is the unabated curiosity in man that has kept the developments going on and evolution of human knowledge expanding.

All events in the universe are cyclic

Although, the formation of basic natural elements and conditions under which they were initially formed, still continues to be a great scientific mystery, it may be understood that all material creations in the universe are not only crystalline but also periodic and cyclic in nature, forming various structures under different conditions and finally breaking up and returning back into the primordial natural elements from which they got formed.

Natural events from rotation of the Earth and Moon around the Sun, annual seasons, vegetative production of all kinds of cereal, flower, fruit and crops, animal reproductions, diurnal cycles of dark and light, biological rhythm and temperature, etc are some of the common cyclic phenomena each responding to the light radiation, thermal flux, molecular stimulation or any other such kind of signals generated by the cyclic changes in the geomagnetic forces of the Earth as well as those of the Sun, Planets, the Moon and terrestrial or combined environmental conditions. William F. Patterson in his famous book- 'Man Weather and Sun '- Springfield, Illinois, Charles C. Thomas, 1947, introduced the concept of Man as a 'Cosmic Resonator' programmed to survive in harmony not only with seasonal cycles of weather but with Sun, Earth and Moon as well. It is now well known that whereas the Sun provides the essential energy to drive all life forms, it is indeed the Moon that sustains the atmosphere and all life forms on the earth and the entire universe is believed to contribute to what we are. Biological cycles reveal themselves in periodic rhythm in hibernation, mating behavior, body temperature, blood structure, its volume, viscosity and pressure besides several other physiological and behavioral processes induced by terrestrial and cosmic disturbances and controlled by correspondingly induced, endogenous hormonal secretions from the hypothalamus, pineal, pituitary and several other glands. The master control that directs human physiology, thoughts and actions is the brain, an elaborate circuitry of over hundred billion inter-connected nerve cells activating transmission and reception of hormonal messages to various organs at a naturally controlled constant temperature. A fluctuating brain temperature leads to erratic and unpredictable reactions and obviously behavior in man, animals and insects. Even plants get stimulation from the environment around them and respond in terms of induced physiological and biochemical changes. It is remarkably puzzling why our bodies and those of most mammals and birds maintain a uniformly constant temperature close to 37.5 degree Celsius irrespective of our living in the Arctic or the African Sahara desert. Therefore, if man wants to live in peace, health and harmony on Earth, he has to understand, follow, and act in accordance with the laws of nature. Any neglect or departure or liberties (*knowingly or ignorantly*) against the natural laws are only known to spell disaster and doom. However, despite inherent capacity, not all human beings attempt to understand, comprehend and resolutely act according to the natural laws (*the true religion*).

Therefore, the teachings and code of conduct given by the pioneers / seers to a common man in so called scriptures of different Spiritual sects of the world, were fundamentally to realize, understand and live scientifically under existing conditions, as per these natural laws. It is the aberrant practice of those pristine teachings by the descendent followers in different environmental and social conditions under banners of organized groups, has created shades of religions in different names and divided humanity into factions. The only religion of human kind is to understand the science and scientific basis of his existence in relation to universal conditions. And it is purely an individualistic pursuit from within own self and physical body. Organized form of any religion (*howsoever benevolent, it may look from outside*) is therefore nothing short of a brute force, promoted, perpetrated, hyped and even enforced by use of muscular force for collective pseudo supremacy / security, born out of fear for losing social patronage and protection, power, position, control, influence, authority, purpose, motive or for any such kind. Christopher Hitchens in his monumental book –'God is not great', has beautifully described how the threat of an eternal punitive hell, a teaching that for centuries had been used to frighten and shock innocent children into believing what their parents or religious leaders did. It is therefore not very surprising that anything said (*even in a spirit of free enquiry*) against such orthodoxy, which has been imprinted and imbibed in the minds of individuals since childhood, for thousands of years should meet criticism, opposition and even rebellion. Religion will not die, says Hitchens, " or until we get over our fear of death, and of the dark, and of the unknown, and of each other and religious coercion of scarring children into belief with the ideas of Hell (*and wrath of GOD*)." Even, Albert Einstein, the celebrated Nobel Physicist, presenting his views on Science, Philosophy and Religion in 1940 says- "A person who is religiously enlightened, appears to me to be one who has, to the best of his ability, liberated himself from the fetters of his selfish desires and is preoccupied with thoughts, feelings and aspirations to which he clings because of their super-personal value." And when once asked straight out if he believed in God, he replied: "I believe in Dutch Philosopher Benedict or Baruch Spinoza's personal God who reveals himself in the orderly harmony of what exists and not in a God who concerns himself with fates and actions of human beings. I cannot conceive of a God who rewards and punishes his creatures." Further, while attempting to define his own religiosity, Einstein emphatically said: "Try and penetrate with our limited means the secrets of nature and you will find that, behind all the discernible concatenations, there remains something subtle, intangible and inexplicable. Veneration for this force (*behind all creation*) beyond anything that we can comprehend is my religion. To that extent I am, in point of fact, religious. The religious geniuses of all ages have been distinguished by this kind of religious feeling, which knows no dogma and no God conceived in man's image; so that there can be no church whose central teachings are based on it. Religion and science meet for the cosmic religious experience, which is the strongest and noblest driving force behind scientific research."

Physical and spiritual realms

According to the Vedic philosophy, there are two principles of reality. Whereas physics, chemistry and for that matter all sciences are within the first category, life belongs to the non-physical spiritual realm governed by the existence of a non-chemical or non-molecular spiritual soul of pure conscious energy and it follows its own spiritual laws. All living bodies are made up of molecules of organic matter; and these bodies are animated by the presence of the soul (*universal consciousness*). Taking analogy of a car and its driver inside, when the driver is away, the car stops and cannot move. Similarly, when the spirit soul goes away / or when death occurs, the body with all its molecular machinery still intact is no longer animated. The presence of the spirit soul is not limited to the human beings alone but all living entities including microbes have spirit souls. This spirit soul, the seed of life, has existed ever since eternity and has been believed to manifest itself (at least in higher living beings) from the moment of conception. The continual connection, distribution, manifestation, operation, auto-generation and symptoms of withdrawal of the soul (*universal consciousness*) can only be observed / searched / probed though the human body, because it is only the man from amongst the animal world with his physical body as an experimental instrument and faculty of mind, can do so as an independent observer.

The periodic cycles of creation and annihilation of material world along with living beings take place continuously like changes of seasons. Four such cycles called by the name Satya, Treta, Dwapara and Kali yuga (Cycle) appear by rotation. I wonder if these four cycles scientifically represent, the periodic time frames of conditions, within which, there is a preponderance / pre-dominance of one of the four fundamental forces of nature over the other three, so that creation, sustenance or destruction of the visible matter (*Maya*) continues gradually in phases, despite their being in simultaneous operation together all the time. This is possibly evident from the example of a star whose iron-rich core, when cross a threshold size of 1.4 solar masses, the gravitational force gains the upper hand to the extent such that the core, under its influence implodes down to the size of a neutron star, releasing tremendous amount of energy to blow off the overlying material in a colossal explosion and creating a supernova. Physical explanation for such eventful cycles will have to be searched. Seeds of Life, either manifested or un-manifested, can embody on earth from any organism– unicellular bacteria, plants, birds, animals or human beings according to the subtle laws of karma (the action) performed by a living entity under the influence of three characteristics of material nature *(gunas)*; 'Sat, Tama and Rajas'. Here again, I wonder if these so called three *gunas,* actually stand to mean (*in modern scientific terms*) and refer to the three kinds of electrovalent, covalent and coordinate nature of chemical bonds that are responsible for the formation, quality and characteristics of the innumerable structures between atoms of different chemical elements to form material compounds of diverse kind. Madame Elisabeth Kubler-Ross has emphatically demonstrated the existence of even cyclic phases in human life death and rebirth, through rigorous scientific experimental work, despite strong reservations against such belief in oriental philosophy between different religions.

Body as a physical laboratory and conditions for success

Science has given technical knowledge, material prosperity and physical comforts to human civilization. However, it needs to be borne in mind that like the disciplines of science and technology, there indeed exists a body of knowledge which disciplines natural tendencies, helps to exercise control over emotions, reins the drifting mind, tames uncontrolled thoughts, restrains from thoughtless actions and leads an individual on the path to seek the real purpose of human life. This knowledge is what is called 'Spirituality'. Spirituality seeks to identify manifestation of the spirit soul (*universal consciousness*) within our own body. It is concerned more with passionate realization through experience from within rather than something happening physical from outside. Human body, under the circumstances, functions as a physical laboratory. And since all scientific experiments (*in material and biological sciences*) need perfect instrumental and environmental conditions to succeed, 'Path to Spirituality' requires essentially tuning the physical body in unison to perceive subtlest signals from the spirit-soul. This tuning therefore must take place, harmoniously according to the natural scientific principles, laws, rules and conditions. There is no denying of the fact that the entire universe indeed, contributes to what we are. All desires, likes, dislikes, passions, tensions, aspirations of the five sensory organs, self-ego, pride and prejudices arising within the mind must be removed. Perfect Control over mind and concentration of thoughts are the keystone of the arch of the gateway to spirituality. Self-ego gets dissolved with cultivation of universal love, affection and humility and self-confidence and fearlessness become the acquired attributes of a spiritually enlightened man. Unfortunately, people erroneously equate spirituality with religion, which most often divides us rather than to agree on a commonality of the purpose of our very existence. In my opinion, the sole purpose of any organized religion should and must have been to only motivate large number of people to follow the path of self-realization, rather than subjecting them to the practice ritualistic traditions in some form or other. A true scientist is as much religious and spiritual as any acknowledged saint from any organized religious group. Laskar Award winner Scientist Madame Candace B. Pert in her celebrated book- 'Molecules of Emotion' emphatically describes with experimental evidence, deeper connection between thoughts, actions and neuropeptides secreted in the brain and body and a quote from her book is illuminating; "All processes that impact on survival- sex, eating, breathing, etc. – are highly regulated by neuropeptides, and thus are emotionally directed. The simple emotions of pain and pleasure, signaling us to move either towards or away from it, have been key determinants in whether an animal or human survives or evolves. Our large and small intestines are densely lined with neuropeptides and receptors, all busily exchanging information laden with emotional content, which we experience. There are at least twenty different emotion laden peptides (*.. are these the precursors of the essential amino acids?)* released by the pancreas to regulate the assimilation or storage of nutrients, all carrying information about satiety and hunger. It is the peptide that mediates satiety and hunger and we cannot hear what our peptides are telling us when we are disconnected from or in denial about, our emotions. Similarly, blood flow is closely regulated by emotional peptides, which signal receptors on blood vessel walls to constrict or dilate, and so influence the amount and velocity of blood flowing through them from moment to moment".

Bhagvad Gita and vedic philosophy are universal

There is no doubt that the oldest philosophy on the earth showing path to seekers in spirituality and the perfect way of living on earth, in tune with the laws of nature is the *Vedic Advaita* Philosophy. And this philosophy is purely scientific in its approach to realization of the ultimate reality based on the principles of natural laws of creation. Vedas are known to were received and imbibed by Maharshis of the Vedic times from the vibrations, sounds, consonants, vowels, words, rhythm, beats and fluxes of energy descended down from the moment of creation and transformed into a language called the 'Sanskrit'. This language was evolved as a combination of various frequencies of vibrations and energies that are running through human being in unison with the cosmic universal consciousness. Each letter is related to a particular form of waveform and different alphabets, when joined together constitute packets / bundles of resultant waves with characteristic frequency and energy content. The 'Sanskrutic' language is therefore inherently superimposed and naturally runs through every human being as an undercurrent, irrespective of his / her personal language, religion, faith, belief, cast, creed or geographic location on the earth. It is therefore no surprise that Sanskrit should have been acknowledged as the mother of most of the Asian and European languages. That is the common thread of reality between all races of human kind (civilized or uncivilized, educated or illiterate) and explains why an object of beauty, a couplet of fine poetry, a passage of compassionate text or a mind-quieting note of musical sound and actions full of love, affection and compassion have universal appeal. There is therefore no giver, author or compiler of the knowledge and wisdom given in the Vedas. The truth in this assertion is evident also from the explicit descend of the Erwin Schrodinger's wave equation from his mind, which was not otherwise possible to derive from anything known; the mathematical equations written with solutions by the Mathematical genius Srinivasa Ramanujam, Kekule's decoding the structure of benzene with six carbon atoms joined together in a hexagonal closed ring from his dream, the theory of general relativity that stemmed from Einstein's deep insight rather than being stimulated or guided by any specific experiment or observation and several such instances are the recent examples of knowledge percolating from somewhere mysteriously unknown.

The manifestation of energy within a human body is mediated through the seven energy centers called the 'chakras' which lie along the spinal chord, in unison with the universal cosmic energy with the help of three energy conduits (*nadis*) named '*Ida*', '*Pingala*' and the '*Sushumna*'. Smooth flow of energy through the charkas is regulated and controlled by the frequency and depth of breathing (*pranayam*). Mind is controlled by rigorous discipline, punctuality, regularity and thoughts and impressions through meditation but actions (*karma*) cannot be done so. Since the seven charkas regulate flow of energy on their turn to various organs, parts and regions of the human body for physical action, any obstruction to this energy flow between charkas is reflected in the form of ailment or disease of an organ under the control of those particular chakras. This is the fundamental natural law for our physical, physiological, metabolic, mental and spiritual health and continued blissful existence on the earth.

There are therefore no other natural laws for people of different cast, creed, colour of the external skin, physical size or location on the earth. Vedic *Advaita* Philosophy is universal in its approach, appeal, contents and practice. It is tragic that it is incorrectly labeled at times by the ignorant as 'Hindu Religious Philosophy'. The 'Vedas, Upanishads, and the Bhagvad Gita' represent the pinnacles of achievement of a holistic science, spirituality and sincere universal guide to those who wish to tread the path of spirituality, healthful living, universal love and salvation into the cosmic consciousness (Moksha). Perhaps the only Universal Religion (as an essential duty) for every one of us is to collectively and individually maintain himself / herself mentally, thoughtfully, physiologically, nutritionally and physically in sound good health, depending upon geographical location on the earth, because food intake, its nature and effective digestion by the body's metabolism are mediated to a great extent by the external environmental conditions and mental strategies (thoughts) to combat them for survival. This is the only meaning of spirituality and essence of the teaching of all religions, past or present that have flourished on earth. No wonder, Madame

Candace B. Pert, a modern *immuno*-pharmacologist, in tune with the Vedic philosophy, attaches great importance to exercising complete control over thoughts, emotions and language for a healthy living. Because, thoughts provoke biosynthesis of peptides, polypeptides, hormones, proteins and enzymes within the brain and body and moderate human physiology and body- actions. And when action is performed, its appropriate logical consequence being a reaction that follows almost immediately. From this point of view, every word that we speak constitutes a 'mantra' and has the inherent capacity to evoke physical action.

Concept and nature of god

No other concept has remained so enigmatic as that of GOD and this has remained with man ever since he learnt to observe, analyze, remember and possibly think and correlate the innumerable natural phenomenon as inter- play of energies, forces and effects, occurring over matter of diverse kinds and taking place around him from somewhere unknown. It is ignorance about possible causes and predominantly the fear (self-generated or induced) about someone unknown imagined to be operating, conducting and destroying the visible nature that created the concept of GOD. And this dogma has remained with the humanity ever since, through thousands of years despite some valiant attempts by scientific pioneers to see relevance on the basis of scientific logic, experience and reason. History is a witness to the torture, humiliation and sentences being given to these pioneers by unreasonable advisors and authorities who ruled over kingdoms. In the absence of a rational system of education, uniformly reasonable level of scientific temper, logic, reason, competence and analytical mind amongst a majority of subjects of all civilizations, GOD has not only remained relevant (or maintained to be so) but has flourished in the hands of the traders, brokers and middlemen of organized religious groups as pseudo links between him (God) and a common man. Many countries of the world have enshrined God in their national constitution and rulers owe allegiance to their constitution in the name of God.

God! If, at all exists, must indeed show off in the form of his profound energy. Scientists are aware that only one tenth of the actual matter constitutes the visible universe and the balance nine tenth, remains as mysteriously invisible and dispersed energy called as the dark matter in the universe. All matter throughout the universe is the outcome of one primordial matter called the ether (*akasha*) and all forces, gravitational or electromagnetic is the outcome of cosmic energy called the (*prana*) cosmic consciousness and action of *prana* on *akasha* creates the universe. It is the Oriental Advaita Vedant Philosophy that not only professed an intimate connection between man and the cosmos, but actually showed a practical way of realizing this through breathing exercises (*pranayam*) and regulation of conscious energy through the seven energy centers called the 'chakras' lying along the spinal cord of the human body. From Einstein's equation of mass-energy equivalence, both mass and energy become true functions of each other and space and time no longer remain absolutes. A God of pure conscious cosmic energy can become a doctrine for Christians or an incarnation (*avatar*) perceived by the Hindus and Tibetan Buddhists. In reality, both religion and orthodox science are indeed founded on faith i.e. belief in the existence of unexplained God outside the universe who governs and brings natural order and unexplained set of physical laws and universal physical constants that keep the cycle of universal creation going on in abstract transcendent realm of perfect mathematical relationships. For this reason therefore, both religion and science do not provide satisfactory explanation for physical existence. And as Paul Davis explains; " for Christians, world depends utterly on God for its existence, while the converse is not the case, so physicists declare a similar asymmetry; the universe is governed by eternal laws (or meta-laws) but the laws are completely impervious to what happens inside the universe. The only possible compromise at present being to consider both the eternal immutable laws or meta-laws of physics and the universe they govern to be part and parcel of a unitary system to be incorporated together within a common explanatory scheme, with explanation coming from within the universe and without appeal to an external agency. Until science comes up with testable theory of laws of the universe, its claim to be free of faith is manifestly bogus."

The *Advait Vedantic* Sages from India emphatically declared that the basic elements do not change but their relevance can do so in relation to spirituality, religiosity, politics, astronomy and modern science etc. It can therefore be inferred that both science and spirituality should be based on a common foundation. Whereas modern science seeks truth in qualitative, quantitative, systematic, experimental, logical and conclusively testable way, although not without limitations, Vedantic approach to truth is sought from within the human body in limitless micro dimension and fathoms much-more deeper than what the modern science does.

References

1. Guney M.R., 'Dnyaneshwari Che Bhava-Vishwa' in Marathi, Snehal Prakashan, Mumbai, 2006, 192p.

2. SAVIJNANAM-Scientific Exploration for a Spiritual Paradigm, Vol 1,2,3-4, Journal of the Bhaktivedanta Institute, Kolkata, Ed. In Chief-Bhaktisvarupa Damodara Swami (Dr. T.D. Singh), 2002, 2003, 2004-

3. 2005 respectively.

4. Parnov E.I., 'At the Crossroads of Infinities, Translated by Vladimir Talmy, MIR Publishers, Moscow, 1974, 397p.

5. Chawn Marcus,'Magic Furnace' Vintage, 2000, 232p.

6. 'Dnyaneshwari and Bhakti Movement', Compendium of eighteen articles by various authors. Published by Maharashtra Information Centre, New Delhi, 1984, 100p.

7. 'HINDU DHARMA-The Universal Way of Life' Voice of the Guru-Pujyasri Chandrasekharendra Sarasvatiswami, Jagadguru, the 68 th Shankaracharya of Kanchi Kamakoti Pitha, Bharatiya Vidya Bhavan, Bombay, 1995, 790p.

8. Segre Gino, 'Einsteins Refrigerator: Tales of Hot and Cold', Allen Lane, Penguine Books, 300p.

9. Pert, Candace B. 'Molecules of Emotion', Pocket Books, London, 1997, Chapter 13, pp 279-315.

10. Gokhale P.V.,'Spand Tatvaavar Adharit Bramha Vidyecha Vidnyan Paath' In Marathi Language, Published by the Author, reprinted edition 2002, 367, Narayan, Laxmi Road, Pune, India.

11. Cowan David with Silk Anne, 'Ancient Energies of the Earth- A ground breaking exploration of the earth's natural energy and how it affects our health'. Thorsons: An Imprint of Harper Collins, 1999, pp319.

12. Emoto Masaru, 'The Hidden Messages in Water' Translated by David A Thayne, Atria Books, 2001 pp 157.

13. Kubler-Ross, Elisabeth. **www.elisabethkublerross.com**

14. Wiley Steven, 'Waiting for Einstein: The dawn of a unified theory of biology may finally be upon us'. The Scientist.com Vol 22 Issue 10, Page 31.

15. Paul Davis, 'Taking science on faith' November 24, 2007 (New York Times); **http://www.rationalvedanta.net/node/155**, the website for western and eastern philosophical and enlightened thoughts. Paul Davis,'The Mind of God-Science and search for ultimate meaning', Penguine Books, 1992.

16. Rees, Martin,'Just Six Numbers' Phoenix Paperback, 1999.

17. Spiridnov,O. P., 'Universal Physical Constants, MIR Publishers, Moscow, 1986.

Our Cosmic Relationships, Development, Structure, Make-Up and Integrity of Human Body, Flow of Energies, Food Nutrition and Good Health: An Attempted Synthesis

Abstract

This comprehensive article is targeted to benefit students and teachers in schools, colleges and universities. All formally educated and self-educated individuals and particularly the young mothers in domestic environments, are expected to benefit from the information given regarding the role of nutrition, nutrient supplementation in daily diet for personal health. The author has attempted to look for a syntheses between the traditional knowledge since time immemorial and the modern scientific concepts on human nutrition and nutrition supplements as are believed to be linked to the twelve Sun–Sign-related 'birth salts' of Homeopathy, correlations of planetary influences on various organs in human body, nutritional requirement of various organs for their efficient functioning in relation to the physical, biological, spiritual and mental health. The perceptions of their relationships are not as simple as have been described in this article. This article is only an attempted synthesis to logically indicate their plausible connections and inter-relations existing at the subtlest level, beyond current understanding of the biochemical reaction-kinetics and physical laws of material and energy flow. The intended message is meant to simply arouse awareness in the younger generation in securing good health under very dynamic, hectic, tense and fiercely competitive life style that has been thrust upon humanity for survival by the globally competitive economic and trade activity.

Introduction

It is well known that the annual 360° degrees 'circular trajectory' of the movement of Earth around the Sun is further subdivided into twelve equal angular arc segments of 30⁰ each with Sun at the centre. These twelve angular arc segments have been arbitrarily named as the twelve 'Sun Signs' thousands of years ago, after imaginary perceptible figures / shapes seen in the visible clusters of galaxies and stars called the constellations. These twelve Sun Signs are given in Table 1 (columns 1, 2, 3).

The International Astronomical Union, since 1929, has grouped all the prominently seen 88 Stellar Constellations within twelve angular segments of the Sun-Signs depending upon their month wise visibility across the Zodiac. Of these 88 Constellations, 10 each are distinctly seen in the months of July and September, 8 each in the months of February, March, April and December; 7 each in the months of May and October; 6 in the months of January and November and only 5 in the months of June and August. These Constellations move so slowly that they would always be found at about the same place within our life time. Constellations vary in their distances, magnitude, luminosity, extent and number of galaxies and stars within every cluster falling in each thirty degree arc segment of the Zodiac. A group of constellations although may appear to lie in the same direction on the horizon, they are not connected to one another. Even inter-star distances within an individual galaxy and between galaxies vary from few to several hundreds of light years. As a result, the energy component of constellations from outer space, particularly in the direction of the Sun of our own galaxy varies considerably from and within each 30⁰ arc segment of the horizon. The energy from the constellations directed towards the Sun within each arc segment of the Zodiac, mixes with the sunlight and the combined modified flux of energy hit the Earth and other planets of the solar system from all directions. Constellations are also the source of radiant energy of the electromagnetic type in various wavelength, frequency and energy bands besides components of highly energetic corpuscular type of cosmic rays. Physicists have identified only four 'Primary Forces' of nature, namely; weak interaction, strong interaction, electro-weak and gravitation, that govern the entire creation, sustenance and destruction of the material creation in the universe.

Moon, the satellite of the Earth, while going round the Earth and across its trajectory around the Sun, does not necessarily face directly the same segment of the Zodiacal Sun-Sign as the Earth. The line joining the centers of Earth and Moon traces different segments of the Zodiac simultaneously depending upon its position relative to the Earth. The position of the Moon across the Zodiac at the time of the birth of man is known as his Moon-sign (Chandra Rashi). Moon sign is considered to be very important in that it conveys the status of the mind, attitude, likes, dislikes, aspirations, nature and desires expressed as per the program inherited on his / her DNA from his parents. 'Charaka Samhita' originally written by Maharshi Charaka, clearly describes that the mental make-up of a child depends upon the mental status of his parents at the time he/she was conceived, the sounds heard repeatedly by the pregnant woman, the memory of the actions encoded on the DNA, inherited from father that results into an embryo and develops into a new individual with particular type of mental, physical and other faculties (New combination of genetic make-up arising out of the combination and fusing of the genes from the mother and father under the influence of the prevalent epigenetic conditions at the time of conception). Vedas list 26 divine qualities and describe the 'Garbhadharan' ceremony of purification to be performed by the parents before conceiving a child to be born with exceptionally good qualities of mind and physical body. Obviously, Moon sign is directly responsible for the mind and the thought processes that continuously churn it. Thoughts, positive or negative on their turn are known to control the physiology, metabolic biochemical reactions and consequently the body actions and mental emotions under their influence. Since, for every action, there is an opposite reaction, all actions performed by an individual invoke their consequences in return. It may also be observed that whereas the Sun provides the necessary energy to propel life processes on the Earth, it is the Moon that sustains the life on it. The thin blanket of the Earth's atmosphere and the cycle of saturation of atmospheric moisture and precipitation are sustained by the Moon. Full appreciation about the effects of Moon on human beings and other life forms and the entire ecosystem, based on scientific data is accumulating fast with the advance of space technology and data gathered from the extra-terrestrial remote sensing probes. Characteristic curative properties to the ingredients of Tibetan Astro-medicines prepared under different phases and obviously energy fluxes of the moon are well known. Similarly Crop-Specific Periods in a calendar year for cultivation of any agricultural crop in any part of the world is in fact linked to the quantum of energy required by it for growth and its availability during that time of the year. The success of the All India

Coordinated Crop Improvement Projects for various cereals, legumes, cotton and oilseeds crops, conceived and launched by the Indian Council of Agricultural Research for ascertaining location specific performance of a particular genotype and its production potential since 1960 was essentially linked to this reality besides other important factors. Much of the credit for the success of the first ever 'Green Revolution' in India in 1967-68 goes to this All India Coordinated Wheat Improvement Project and its Project Coordinator Dr. Atmaram Bhairav (A.B.) Joshi.

Like the Moon, the line joining the centers of the Earth and other planets of our solar system, face different Sun signs during their transit around the Sun. The energy fluxes from the outer galaxies and space modified by them with the Sun have considerable influence on the general life of an individual on the earth. An irrevocable evidence of the effect of Mars and other planets and correlation with vocational profession of individuals was shown by a French Astronomer Michael Gauqueline in 1950 and later by a German Astronomer Suitbert Ertel. According to Sharad Upadhey, Professor of Astrology from India, whereas the Sun affects the developing fetus in emergence and growth of various organs in human body; energy from the Moon creates and controls the neuronal activity and consequently the mind; Mercury affects voice, the intellect and wisdom; Jupiter has effect on reasoning; Venus affects the sperm, faculties of love, art, music and society; Saturn the sensitivity of the heart and all muscular actions are affected by the planet Mars. The twelve Zodiac signs and their ruling planets (Table-1,column 4) have also been associated with the twelve important parts of a human body as; Aries with Forehead; Taurus with the Mouth; Gemini with the Chest area; Cancer with the Heart; Leo with the Stomach; Virgo with the Waist; Libra with the Bladder; Scorpio with the Sex Organ; Sagittarius with the Thighs; Capricorn with the Knees and Knee joints; Aquarius with the Calf Muscle of the Legs and Pisces with the Feet of human body.

Sun signs have also been associated with dominant effects of the chemical salts of elements such as Sodium, Potassium, Calcium, Iron, Magnesium and Silica, which are essential for the metabolic functioning and survival of human bodies as healthy units. Phosphate, sulphate and chloride salts of the above elements are called the Birth-Salts of individuals. Table-1, column 5, lists the birth salts by chemical composition and by their name (in brackets) in Homeopathy, depending upon the Sun sign Table-1, column 3. It may be interesting to note that salts of Calcium, Iron, Potassium, Sodium and Magnesium are essentially required by various organs of the human body for effective growth and functioning of bones, teeth, blood, tissue, nerves, muscles, skin, arteries and bone marrow. Practitioners of Homeopathy claim that pills of birth salts of 200X potency, taken regularly by an individual on his birthday, keeps him healthy throughout the year with vigour and vitality. Although it is extremely difficult to precisely delineate the correlation of the Sun sign with Birth Salts and vitality of individual physiology, the cosmic forces and their resonance at the time of birth under a particular Sun sign has something to do both with excitation energy of Birth Salts in tune with cyclic repetition of natural characteristic frequencies and energies of the fused sperm and ovum cells together for conception. It may be remembered that these salts are crystalline in their structure and composition and have characteristic frequencies / wavelengths at which they absorb or transmit radiations in solution or in crystalline forms. This also seems logical because all creations in the universe are not only crystalline but periodic and cyclic in nature forming various structures under different conditions and finally breaking up and returning back into the natural elements from which they got formed. Natural events from rotation of the Earth and Moon around Sun, annual seasons, vegetative production of all kinds of cereal, fruit and flower bearing crops, animal reproductions, diurnal cycles of dark and light, biological rhythm and temperature etc are some of the common cyclic phenomena each responding to the radiation signals generated by the cyclical changes in the geomagnetic forces of the Earth as well as those of the Sun, Planets, the Moon and terrestrial or combined environmental conditions. William F. Patterson in his famous book- 'Man Weather and Sun'- Springfield, Illinois, Charles C. Thomas, 1947 introduced the concept of Man as a 'Cosmic Resonator' programmed to survive in harmony not only with seasonal cycles of weather but with Sun, Earth and Moon as well. Biological cycles reveal themselves in rhythm in hibernation, mating behaviour, body temperature, blood- pressure, structure and volume and in several other physiological processes controlled by endogenous hormonal secretions.

It is well known that 71% of the surface on Earth is covered by water and only 29 % by land. Surprisingly, our bodies and even those of all the living beings on Earth have the same proportion i.e. 71% water and 29% matter and therefore the Moon, the closest of the heavenly bodies has considerable effects on the living beings. It may be interesting to note that chloride, fluoride, phosphate and sulphate salts of calcium, magnesium, sodium, iron and potassium constituting the birth salts of those born in the twelve Sun signs are also the physical requirements for effective functioning of human and animal metabolisms. Since the Sun sign periods are overlapping between consecutive calendar months of a year, the combination of Birth Salts of two consecutive Sun signs would be equally beneficial to those born in between the two signs.

Each part of the human body is made up of a specific organ which in turn is essentially powered by the pre-dominant ionic exchange of particular element, required for its function. Any malfunctioning of an organ is fundamentally linked to restriction to the flow / exchange of the ions / energy and such malfunctioning can be rectified through the supply of such specific ions or nutrition to the organ in minute quantities in molecular exchangeable forms. Dietary minerals are naturally extracted by the plants from the soil and plants are consumed by humans and animals directly or indirectly. Calcium occurs mainly in teeth, bones and in blood plasma and other body fluids influencing nerve transmission, blood clotting and muscle contraction. Calcium is best absorbed by the body in association with vitamin D. Phosphorus is present in every individual cell in compounds such as nucleic acids and adenosine triphosphate (ATP) molecules. Phosphorus is closely allied to calcium in teeth and bones. Magnesium is also present in every cell and is essentially required for carbohydrate and protein synthesis, cell reproduction and smooth muscular actions. Sodium a component of extra cellular fluid maintains the critical acid-base balance, ionic permeability across cell membranes and in muscle functions. Potassium, found in intra and extra cellular fluid, plays a major role in maintaining fluid and electrolyte balance, in heart muscle activities, in carbohydrate metabolism and protein synthesis. Chlorine, a constituent of extra cellular fluid along with Sodium, maintains fluid-electrolyte and acid-base balance. Chlorine, in the form of hydrochloric acid is present in the stomach where it provides an acidic environment for breaking up the food constituents for easy digestion. Sulfur, an important constituent of all proteins is necessary for energy metabolism, enzymatic functions and detoxification. Other minerals such as Iron, Iodine, Cobalt, Chromium, Copper, Fluorine, Manganese, Molybdenum, Selenium and Zinc are also required by human body in the synthesis of essential metabolites.

Requirement for other minerals such as Boron, Nickel, Silicon, Vanadium, Bismuth, Rubidium, Tellurium, Titanium, Tungsten, Strontium by the human body has also been reported but not experimentally confirmed to certainty.

Practically, it is immaterial whether nutritional supplementation is carried out through kind of chemical formulations under various systems of Ayurvedic, Chinese, Tibetan, Unani, and Homeopathic or Allopathic brand names. The most essential point being that the targeted supplementation is adequate in quantity and effectively assimilated by the body or the particular organ in the shortest possible time. This is probably the reason why specific formulations of nutrition supplements, formulated and marketed under all the established systems of medicines are potentially effective against one or the other metabolic disorder. No wonder, we find a large number of persons including medical physicians reposing their faith in all these forms of medicinal systems. It is tragic that the practitioners of these systems, instead of experimentally verifying and complementing each other are very often dogmatic and look down upon the other with contempt and suspicion.

It is worth remembering that all systems of medicines were evolved in different parts of the world and in different geo-climatic and ecological environments. The formulations of nutritional supplements prepared, marketed and administered were perhaps the best compromise at that time depending upon the knowledge about the availability and source of the required ingredients. The purpose and objective of all systems of medicine is to supply proper nutrition to the affected part of the body or its organ and definitely there is no conflict for supremacy of one system over the other.

What is true about the linkage of nutritional supplementation with functions of a body organ, is equally true about the supplementation of the essential amino acids, proteins, enzymes, hormones and vitamins that carry out the most intricate and exhaustive functions of our metabolism and immune systems efficiently. The master control that directs human thoughts and actions is the brain, an elaborate circuitry of over hundred billion interconnected nerve cells activating transmission and reception of signals of hormonal messages to various organs at a naturally controlled constant temperature. A fluctuating brain temperature (in case of severe infections) leads to erratic and unpredictable reactions. Mineral and nutritional supplementation of human body therefore lies at the base of healthy functional tissues, nerves, bones, muscles and cells of various organs. Prolonged imbalance in any of the various normal dietary nutritional components can lead to causation of various forms of cancer, cardiovascular diseases, Parkinson disease, paralysis, and disorder of secretion glands, function of kidneys and cataract of the eye lens.

Most essential nutrients are required in small quantities and are usually stored and re-used by the body. As a result, unlike the urge sensed immediately by the body for water and oxygen rich fresh air, the absence of essential nutrients usually takes long time to lead to the development of symptoms and dietary deficiency linked diseases. In the process an individual is often caught unaware to fall an easy prey to diseases of various kinds.

Voluntary nutritional supplementation by all the 'health-conscious' enlightened individuals is therefore an Insurance Policy that will ensure and deliver maturity benefits of health, vigour, vitality and freedom from diseases in life only to yourself than to your nominees. Any compromise or neglect on this account due to constraints on money or time can be disastrous in later part of the life.

Whereas appropriate intake levels of each dietary mineral must be sustained to maintain good physical health, excessive intake of dietary minerals, proteins or vitamins may also lead to toxicity and illness directly or indirectly. In large doses, some vitamins have been documented to cause temporary vitamin poisoning with side effects such as nausea; diarrhea and vomiting particularly from the vitamin supplement formulations and can be reverted back with reduction of doses. Over dose of Iron for example, leads to excessive production of free radicals beyond the handling capacity of the antioxidant system of the body with consequent removal of Copper. Like wise, some nutrients need the presence of other for their efficient absorption by the body. High protein, high phosphate foods and vitamin K deficiency cause increased excretion of Calcium from the body through urine. Free radicals get easily formed when a covalent bond between entities gets broken with one electron remaining with each of the newly formed atom. As a result, Free radicals are very highly reactive and form a chain of highly damaging super oxide radicals via electron escape with consumption of oxygen and increasing the rate of metabolic reactions several folds. In the absence of adequate endogenous antioxidant supplementation, the body suffers severe damage to muscles and recovery under normal circumstances may take a long time. In view of these considerations, the best strategy for comprehensive nutrition would be to periodically rotate nutritional supplementation with time gaps or vary according to the physical condition and age of the individual.

Since the science of health and wellbeing today is focused more on prevention and control than cure of diseases in securing good health for a majority of human population, the role of dietary nutrition need not be over emphasized. Eastern and particularly the Indian wisdom since time immemorial say that for healthy living, one has to align himself with the flow of the universe because almost all diseases are due to the patients being out of balance with the laws that govern it. It is here lays the intimate connection between man and the cosmic universe of which he is an integral part. Man has adopted himself for survival on various kinds of diet depending upon geographic location, climatic conditions and availability of flora and fauna. Excessive economic greed, commercialization, diversification in product range, processing and preservation technologies, vigorous marketing, breach of traditional market barriers, consumer preference, alarming growth in human population, very hectic life styles and increasing dependence on processed and preserved food for survival, have changed the strategy of securing healthy living in almost all countries of the world. It is therefore very likely that a food nutritional supplement found effective to a person living in tropical climatic locations may not do so for the one living in desert or freezing climatic conditions and vice versa. This point is important to be noted because food intake and its effective digestion by the body's metabolism are mediated to a great extent by the external environmental conditions and mental strategies to combat them for survival.

Human body constitutes extremely complex and intricately delicate systems with wonderfully coordinated physical movements, food digestion and immunity for defense against diseases, pathological infection and adaptation to sudden changes in external environmental conditions. All of these being initiated by the various glands and controlled through chemical reactions of innumerable kind, transport of chemical ions, radicals, molecule of gaseous elements and flow of electrical energy across cell membranes of individual tissues, muscles, nerves and organelles. Taking only temperature as an example, it is remarkably puzzling why our bodies and those of most mammals and birds maintain a uniformly constant average daily temperature close to 37.5 degrees Celsius irrespective of our living in the Arctic or the African Sahara desert. It is believed that hypothalamus, a tiny organ located deep inside the brain sets the temperature thermostat, controls secretions and dictates many of the key metabolic functions by adjusting water, sugar and fat levels in our body besides guiding the release of hormones which inhibit and enhance our activities. The outer skin is believed to be directly in connection with the hypothalamus through peripheral nervous system and the underlying capillary blood vessels. Signals from these two sources are integrated in the thermoregulatory section of the hypothalamus with simultaneous secretion of hormones to control retention or dissipation of heat in the body system. Signals to brain suggest behavioral changes for immediate action like shedding or putting on more clothes on the person. Whereas, internal temperature varies between organs depending upon the nature of metabolism and the rate and amount of blood flow, liver is recognized to be the hottest organ maintaining temperature close to 40.5 degree Celsius followed by the heart pumping blood through the veins and arteries. All these variations can be distinctly seen and marked with the help of thermal infrared photography. The night vision binoculars used by the armies in detecting intrusion are indeed based on these realties.

Business of formulation and manufacture of nutritional supplements with proper blend of antioxidants, vitamins and amino acids is therefore not an easy task. It requires a back up from scientifically and academically oriented, critical, skillful, dedicated and high caliber team of multi-disciplinary scientists. It is left to the discretion of the reader to find out which organization qualifies this requirement for reposing confidence in the quality of their products.

Sunlight is known to consist of electromagnetic radiations of seven visible colours of characteristic wavelength and frequencies. Since all these colours originate from the fire, they make up for the unbalanced component of it within a body and restore health by stimulating pituitary and pineal glands and regulating hormones. Colours of all shades have been emphatically demonstrated to be stimulating various functions in human body such as mood, temper, relaxation, liver, digestion, kidney, appetite and memory. No wonder, use of colours in everyday life has become extremely important in invoking positive reactions from our surroundings and from those we interact with. Similarly, characteristic molecules of odours and aromas of various substances including flowers also stimulate sensations, secretions from various glands and physiological and biochemical metabolism through the olfactory nerves and tissues, both colour and aroma therapies today have become the complementary part of the Wellness Industry and those affected are deriving relief to a large extent.

Human beings have been known to exist since thousands of years on the physical, the emotional and the spiritual levels. These three levels are not only inter-related but are equally important for total health of an individual. Imbalance or deficiency of any kind in any one of these levels is reflected back in the form of mental, physical or spiritual sickness. Whereas, Spiritual level demands a happy and positive attitude under any situation, emotional level demands thorough control over mind, emotions and thoughts and the physical level demands to be cool and composed in all our actions. The three levels also constitute the cardinal principles for healthy living on the Earth and most of the enlightened people from all countries of the world are not only subscribing to this philosophy but are voluntarily coming forward to propagate it. It is the conviction of the author of this article that promotion of these three cardinal principles should not be left only to the preachers of various religions but must form the first lesson in every household, school, college and university before anything else is taught to a child or student as a conscious moral responsibility of both the parents and the teachers alike. As enlightened citizens responsible for shaping the destiny of future generations, let us join hands together in spreading awareness about nutrition to secure wellness for millions of malnourished children and individuals who live in this country.

The article is based on the information contained in the following books and references;

1. 'Rashi Chakra' (Cycle of Sun signs) in Marathi By Sharad Upadhey, Ranga Bahar, Mumbai, 1997, pp 216.

2. 'Tumchey Rog Barey Karnaari Bara Aaushadhe' (Twelve Medicines that cure your Diseses) in Marathi, D.S. Deodhar, Raghuvanshi Prakashan, Mumbai, pp 71.

3. 'Uapaya Tumchaya Haataat' (Remedy lays in your hands) in Marathi, By Malati Joshi, Ruchi Prakashan, Mumbai, 2003, pp 98.

4. 'Future Youth, How to reverse the ageing process' Edited by Carol Keough, Rajendra Publishing House Pvt. Ltd., Bombay, Indian Edition, 1994, pp 646.

5. 'Back to the Nature for Healthy Living' By A.P. Dewan, A. C. Publishers Pvt. Ltd, In association with the Nature and Yoga Health Centre, Servants of People Society, New Delhi, 1996, pp 189.

6. 'The Power of Colour' By Morton Walker, B. Jain Publishers Pvt. Ltd, New Delhi, 1998, pp 180.

7. 'Einstein's Refrigerator: Tales of Hot and Cold', By Gino Segre, Allen Lane, Penguine Books, 2002, pp 300.

8. 'Magic Furnace' By Marcus Chown, Vintage, 2000, pp 232.

9. 'Epigenetic regulation of protein biosynthesis by scale resonance' By Sternheimer Joel, 1993, Lecture, Kanagawa Science Academy and Teikyo Hospital, Tokyo, May 20.

10. 'The effects of sound on living organisms: Applications in agriculture' By Yannick Van Doorne, Ecosonic, BP 27, 01400 Chatillon Sur Chalaronne, France.

11. E-mail <yannick.vd@club-internet.fr>.

12. 'Under the weather-How the weather and climate affect our health' By Pat Thomas, 2004, Fusion Press & Division of Satin Publications Ltd. London, pp 258.

CHAPTER – 3

Towards Fostering and Building a New World Religion: The Most Scientific 'Sanatan Vedic Philosophy' is the Only Option before Humanity for Peace, Progress, Salvation and Continued Peaceful Existence on Earth

Introduction and historical facts

The adherents of so called 'Sanatan Dharma' or 'Hinduism' for the western world are a part of the oldest documented and continued civilization on the Earth that dates back to at least 25,000 years before Christian era. There certainly was no 'religion' as we imagine from the point of view of the current understanding and definition of terminology. Why I say so, because there is no mention of this kind of concept in any of the oldest scriptures we have inherited. There is only a definition of a certain way of living and we recognize it, by the 'Advait (non-duality) Philosophy' or simply the 'Vedic Philosophy'. And this philosophy for healthful living on Earth, is perennially relevant over any time scale, past, present and future. It is also known by the name as the 'Sanatan (continuing) Dharma'. 'Ved', the oldest documented scriptures in the world are factually the scientific treatises. They talk nothing about 'religion' but only about science, the origin of the Universe and of life on earth including that of man, their position in relation to the universal scheme of creation and about the healthy ways for blissful mutual survival, under continuously changing fluxes of terrestrial, galactic and cosmic energies *(invisible)* in which all life-forms on earth are physically submerged. In reality, we constitute a miniscule speck of dust in the vast expanse of the universal creation. The 'Rishis' of the Vedic civilization have given to mankind the basic knowledge and understanding about geography, astronomy, decimal mathematics, Ayurveda for medical remedies, concepts of medical and plastic surgeries, language and grammar, practicing principles of integrated agriculture and art and science of blending consonents of language alphabets in to Divine Musical compositions called the 'Ragas', expressing various moods to sooth and calm the agitated human mind. And more than these, the complete and comprehensive science of the human body in the 'Yog Sutra/ Shastra' by Sage Patanjali, forms the pinnacle of Vedic Science. In short, the scientific Vedic Philosophy has given to mankind everything it needs for leading a healthy life on the planet Earth. These cardinal scientific principles for healthful living are common to every individual human being. In short, there is no scope and reason for compromising the teachings of '*Sanatan Vedic*' principles and thoughts on account of any pretext. The entire humanity is connected together through only four major 'blood groups and their sub-groups' and by an identical process of coming to birth as a human being and then perishing in death. These processes do not differ on account of colour of the skin, nationality, geographic location on Earth or on the basis of superficially adopted and practiced religious faiths and their rituals.

In contrast, if you dispassionately and judiciously retrospect, without any kind of bias, dogma or concession, the new religious philosophies and the conditions under which they came into being, such as Christianity, Judaism and Islam have given to mankind nothing more than domination, wars, strife, regimentation, fanaticism, jealousy, concept and idea of religious pseudo-supremacy, orthodoxy, regimentally dogmatic practices of outdated, unscientific, religious philosophies, means and methods of appeasement, practice of trading in 'human slaves' and most dangerously the religious sanctity and permissions for committing organized genocides for forcible conversion of people to their respective faiths. They have infused only fear in the minds of followers about the wrath of their *(otherwise benevolent and kind)* respective Gods. In about two thousand years of their emergence, both these organized religious philosophies have physically exterminated the original habitants of several countries from several continents, who were following their own native faith, beliefs and rituals to take control of their countries and sadistically destroying all their places of worship, monuments and identities. The barbarian, extremist and cruel rulers and political masters, under the garb of religion, supported such vandalism for their territorial expansionist designs. Mr. Sanjay Dixit, from his comparative study of these major religions of the world in his book ('All Religions Are Not The Same', Garuda Prakashan, 2023, *pp* 187, ISBN: 979-8-88575-141-4, Gurugram, Bharat) has scholarly summarized the basic principles of all these Abrahamic religions and I quote them verbatim here as mentioned: "Only God, Prophetism; Creationism with concept of Original Sin; Rule of Commandments; Satan as the antithesis of God; Binary Logic; Word of the Book being the Only Truth and the Only Proof; Jesus as the Only Saviour-Redeemption, Resurrection, Ascension; Day of Last Judgement; Eternal Heaven and Hell; We are saved from eternal damnation not by our actions but only with our belief that Jesus is the one true God and he is the only way to Heaven, the Salvation; It is the God-given duty of all Christians to save all the souls in the world from perishing, therefore proselytize; No Sin in killing Non-Believers as they are devil worshippers- False God Syndrome; Church as the enforcer of all of the above and more, its Mandate and Mission. Christianity added some of its own dogma towards the end of the first century of the Common Era. It added the New Testament to the Tanakh, and called it the Bible, now popular as the Judeo-Christian Bible, added a messiah figure and labelled him as the Christ as the Son of God". This is the reason why coronations of Kings, Queens and Nobilities in countries, where they still exist today as the heads of governments, and had adopted Christianity as their State Religion, are performed under the direction of the Church. And during such Coronation processes, the clergies from the Church, conducting the proceedings, assure and reassure by seeking promises for themselves, the protection from the newly crowned kings and queens. In short, the 'Judeo-Christian Bible' is a framed handiwork of a few, who wished to enslave populations and control territories in the name of a 'Dogmatic Belief System' called Christianity. The story of the 'Islam' is almost parallel to this with some modifications from Christianity and Judaism. Sanjay Dixit has again summarized the basic principles of Islam and I quote him verbatim as: "Only God; Prophetism; Creationism with the 'testing' of the created; Satan as permanent rival of Allah; Rule by precepts of the Qur'an; Binary logic; Word of the Revealed Book being the Only Truth and only proof; Allah is the only God worth worshipping; Day of Last Judgement (Akhirat, Qayamat); Eternal Heaven and Health; Heaven (Jannat/Jannah) in after life is only objective; Allah's grace alone can grant Jannah; Whole world to be converted to Islam before Qayamat (Quran 8.39); Holy War (Jihad) a must for every believer (Qur'an 9.123); Mohammad as the 'Final Prophet'; Mohammad as the perfect example to follow (Quran 33.21); All Rights belong only to Allah (of sole worship, being feared and having believers as slaves) and finally; Jihad as Total War". After Islam came into Arabia, they leveraged their position between the conflicting Sassanians (*Iranian*) and Byzantines (*Roman*) to control large swathes of territory and using their 'Doctrine of Jihad' converted all people from the concurred territories, in almost the same way as did the Christians in other parts of the world before them. Therefore, "violence comes very naturally to the 'One God' and the 'Only God' religions who are not loathe to impose their worldview on others. The meditative nature of the 'Sanatan Dharma' with an 'In- Built Inquiry System' is naturally more accommodative and tolerant because 'all systems based purely, on blind belief' seek to dominate and subjugate Nature, natural talent, diversities and creativities. On the other hand, 'inquiry systems' try to seek the fundamentally inherent harmony with Nature." (Sanjay Dixit). Such an 'inquiry system' is only available, supported, professed and practiced by the adherents of the 'Sanatan Dharma Philosophy' and no other faiths or religions.

Contrary to these, Vedic '*Sanatan Dharma*' (way of living), imposes no such restriction, compulsion of even going to temples or following any ritualistic practices. It only invokes people to go within their personal self, practice meditation, learn to keep control over breath and thoughts and seek peace, happiness, tranquility and bliss. It is a historical fact that regimented imposition and adherence to Christian doctrines were vehemently opposed even by early scientific philosophers, thinkers and educated masses and the Church authorities were forced to correct themselves and selectively reform their teachings on 'Christianity' with time and progress of human knowledge. Even Sir Isaac Newton, a celebrated scientist, at the fag- end of his scientific career, had intentionally taken to preaching religion, solely with the purpose of reforming the way it *(Christianity)* was being practiced in those times. But all small changes were done after thousands of innocent people who opposed the views of the Church authorities were massacred and many were forced to drink poison and accept death for defying the 'obstinate', 'dogmatic' and most 'unscientific views' of the Church authorities. The Church authorities had to finally yield and accept the guilt of the actions of their authorities for centuries in the past at the dawn of the twenty first century. They conducted, re-trials of all those, who were convicted and done to death for centuries in the past. This realization and action on the part of the Vatican, is a clear proof and admission of the totally arbitrary, coercive and dogmatic nature of the way Christianity was brutally practiced for centuries in the past. However, in relative comparison, the preachers of Islam from almost all over the world have learnt no such lesson and they continue to remain vehemently rigid and dogmatic despite, visible and glaring contradictions of their philosophy and physical reality established on scientific truth. Unfortunately, they are still resorting to wielding weapons, individual and collective jihadi practices for spreading their organized religion. Practicing and teaching of philosophies based on two thousand years old 'Closed and non-changeable 'meta-narrative' books such as the 'Bible' or the 'Qur'an' appear to have no future in the twenty first century and beyond. Nobody can continue to keep people perpetually ignorant, illiterate and mentally bound to irrelevant, redundant and unscientific thoughts, ideals and practices, particularly in the science and technology driven twenty first century and beyond. No surprise, today, even in countries such as Greece, UK, France, Germany and USA, which were at one time the strongest supporters and observers of ritualistic Christianity, the number of regular church goers for Sunday prayers has dwindled to not more than one to twenty percent depending on age groups. There is a growing influence of atheism and disenchantment about the unscientific philosophies and practice of religion, which is intellectually not stimulating and appealing to the young generations, following rapid developments in science, technology and their practical applications in easing human life. In contrast, the percentage of population attending regular religious prayer in Mosques in almost all the Islamic countries, continue to be over 70-80 percent. All these Islamic countries are known to be economically, scientifically and technologically backward with overall literacy not more than 15-30 percent. This brings out very clearly, that illiterate populations are easier to be manipulated and emotionally blackmailed by religious fundamentalism. Interestingly, voting percentage of such illiterate populations during national elections in their respective countries is well above 80 to 90 percent. Such *en masse* voting patterns are seriously changing the demographic equations in countries where they are migrating in large numbers. No surprise, continued low literacy and the 'orthodox Madarsa-education' amongst the Islamic population serves and suits the purpose of their extremist religious leaders in promoting their goals for furthering demographic changes and expansion for control over resources and populations.

Maintaining elected democratic governments in most countries have come to hang at the pleasure and mercy of the Muslim voters there.

"A 'true religion' is to be understood and lived and not propagated through hired batches of missionaries. It is for the benefit of the entire humanity and is not the monopoly of a group of people or the favoured few or any sect. Religion can never be inherited like property or title. Similarly, it cannot be bestowed upon by a Guru, master, preacher or teacher. It cannot be given or accepted as a gift. If any religion creates class or colour distinctions, barriers between man and man, divides cohesive communities, upholds racial or religious superiority, suffers colour prejudice, tolerates domination of one race, country or nation over another on account of religion or faith, then know for certain that it is not a religion". (G. K. Pradhan in his book-'Know Thyself', Bharatiya Vidya Bhavan, Mumbai, 2015, page 295 (5th edition), *pp* 319.)

Climatic and environmental conditions are the basis of the practice of religion or dharma

Everyone today is aware of the fact that climatic conditions from one location on earth are entirely different from those at other locations. The axial tilt of the polar axis of Earth, constant spinning around this axis and simultaneous elliptically circular rotation around the Sun, bring about such climatic variations. Climates in the Sahara Desert, Arctic and Antarctic, mountainous heights to the plains of tropical and sub-tropical regions are entirely different from one another. This obviously implies that survival strategies under constantly changing environmental conditions in all these locations mentioned above, for any kind of living organism *(human, animal, insect, birds, trees, plants and other kinds of vegetation)* **cannot** be similar. Every living organism will have to fight, evolve, adjust both physically, physiologically and adopt itself to develop the necessary capacity for its survival with good health. This process of evolution for survival under certain specific climatic conditions involves an in-built mechanism of the living organisms to quickly change its physical, physiological, psychological, biochemical and mental state of mind. It must learn to do so by reading the minutest and subtlest signals of changes coming from its surrounding and to take appropriate decision for adaptation.

Any mistake or delay in this process, in all probabilities will be fatal. The 'Survival Strategy' mentioned in the above paragraph is factually the 'Dharma' as has been defined by the Oriental *'Sanatan Vedic'* philosophy. The methods, actions used by the surviving organisms under various climatic conditions, therefore become the part of the 'Rituals' which must go parallel with each other. Obviously, it would be foolish for any species, surviving in Sahara desert to obstinately / dogmatically adhere itself to the same survival strategies, if by chance it happens to be relocated in the arctic or the high altitude mountainous location. My intuition and logic suggests that the whole 'Dharma' of the species must necessarily change instantly with the moment it finds itself relocated from Sahara to a high altitude mountain. If it does not quickly adopt and change to its new 'Dharma', in accordance with the natural environmental conditions at the new location, it has no chances to survive. This is the way all kinds of 'location-specificities' between animals, plants, trees, marine and aquatic organisms, micro-organisms and humans have evolved and stabilized on the Earth since millions of years. 'Dharma' for any living species is therefore not stagnant or rigid ritualistic way but a flexible, dynamically changing strategy for adaptation and survival under constantly changing environmental, epigenetic and morpho-genetic conditions on Earth. No wonder why Rajneesh 'OSHO' had said –"Any religion which does not change according to the new developments in science, technology and social changes and acceptance, has no option but to die."

The spread of the *'Sanatan Vedic'* philosophy *(as a truly scientific way of healthful living on the planet Earth)* from India to several surrounding countries like Sikkim, Bhutan, Nepal, China, Afghanistan, Mynmar (Burma), Ceylon (Srilanka), Thailand, Indoneshia, Malyasia, and even to Arabian countries because of its very scientific foundations had influenced the habitants of these areas for thousands of years. It had even led to new thinking, introspection, comparisons, evaluations, demonstration of implicit results, and adoption with reference to specific local variations and interpretations. No surprise, fundamental tenets of the Vedic philosophy can be explicitly seen as the under-current of almost all the new world religious and philosophies prevalent today, like Buddhism, Jainism, Christianity, Bahaism, Zorastrianism, and Islam, that have originated either from within India or only from places lying geographically close to the Indian Sub-continent. In this context and in my personal considered opinion, I do not consider Sikhism as a separate religion but a sect of the original Vedic Philosophy, that was conspicuously and exclusively raised with a conviction, faith, pledge and determination for the purpose of protecting the *Sanatan Vedic* civilization from the illiterate, uncivilized, barbaric, uncultured invaders from the West, waiting for opportunities to breach the Indian border.

Western concept of religion and sanatan dharma are not the same thing

The concept of 'Religion' has been raised by the westerners and it is not the same as the concept of 'Dharma' from the Vedic philosophy. Religion is an organized and ritualistic practice by a group of people in a mass congregation, essentially exhibiting collective solidarity for geographical and political cohesion. 'Dharma' is purely an independent, personal and subjective strategy for survival (it is always an individual battle for survival against perpetually fluctuating natural epigenetic and surrounding environmental conditions). The word 'Dharma' has been formed from its root – *'Dhru'* or *'Dhr'* meaning- holding together in consonance with the laws of nature. *(The author of this article has explained the factual reality of this statement in his innovative and first of its kind book –A Scientific Look at the Concepts of Soul, Rebirth, Work and the Law of Karma: An Attempted Synthesis, Zorba Books, 2019, pp 136, Chapter 3).* Although general physical, physiological, psychological and biological principles for the working of human bodies irrespective of cast creed, race, colour of skin and nationalities are similar, yet, every individual human being is epigenetically different from the other in every respect of individual characteristics.

All 'Organized 'Religions' require a central authority to oversee the spread of their influence, authority and power over large section of population of followers almost unconditionally. It may be necessary here to bring to the notice of the readers that both Christianity and Islam, as organized religious groups were spread on the might of the swords, threats, coercion, regimentation, blackmail and exploitation of the poor, needy, hungry and diseased persons by purchasing their loyalty in exchange for medical treatment, monetary help, free education and charity with the pre- condition to convert to their faith. The tenets of organized religions were used as tools for political opportunism and control over masses and geographical territories. The very fact that several sagacious and scientifically oriented individuals preferred to drink poison than to subject themselves to the unscientific dogmatic thoughts of Biblical teachings is a glaring proof of the inadequacy of Biblical philosophy and for that matter also that of the Islamic Qur'an, because both of have a common origin. By no means, voluntary acceptance of the teachings of both these organized religions was ever left to the personal choice, preference, intellectual or emotional appeal or self-convincing decision of individuals. Moreover, both Christianity and Islam are the only religions in the world which, consider the non-followers of their religion as sinners and advocates their followers to eliminate them as their fundamental duty. No other religion in the world has such inhuman, intolerant and unkind ingredients in their tenets. On the contrary, there is not a single example in the history of over 25,000 years of the '*Sanatan Vedic*' Civilization (P. V. Vartak), where physical force, or exploitation of ignorance, illiteracy, poverty, diseases have been used with offers of charity for conversion of people in the fold of the '*Sanatan Vedic Dharma*'. The '*Sanatan Dharma*' truly believes in the personal liberty, human right, and his/her own freedom and right to lead their life in the way they want, without interference from anyone. And there are, ample number of evidences from the historical past and present to prove that the promoters of both Christianity and Islam are only dreaming, scheming and aiming to wipe every other faith (or beliefs) with vengeance. They have systematically put mechanisms, checks and counter checks in place, not to allow anyone to revert to his original belief, once he / she is trapped in their fold. And intuitively, I feel that any scheme, which is fundamentally opposed to the inner urge and craving for personal liberty and freedom of human spirit will never succeed.

How, I wish the Scientists and Scientific communities from all over the world dispassionately discuss, without bias, prejudice, or belief at the back of their minds whether there is any need or place for a religion in Human Life? If it is yes, then what should be the essential purpose and cardinal tenets of that religion? And if the only purpose of the religion in human life is to make his/her life cohesive, smooth, free of any kind of mental and physical tensions then analyze as to what extent the current regimental practices (both open and clandestinely hidden) of extending the demographic geographical boundaries under Christianity or Islam are morally justified and ethically free from suppression of human dignity, rights and freedom?

References

1. A V Moharir 'A Scientific Look at the Concepts of Soul, Rebirth, Work and the Law of Karma: An Attempted Synthesis, Zorba Books, 2019, *pp* 136, ISBN 978-93-88497-84-8

2. Sanjay Dixit, 'All Religions Are Not The Same', Garuda Prakashan, 2023, *pp* 187, ISBN: 979-8-88575-141-4, Gurugram, Bharat.

3. G. K. Pradhan in his book- 'Know Thyself', Bharatiya Vidya Bhavan, Mumbai, 2015, page 295 (5th edition), *pp* 319.

4. P.V. Vartak, 'Essays on the Vedic Culture and Literature' (A Felicitation Volume) Blue Bird (India) Ltd, 2007, *pp* 680.

CHAPTER – 4

A Scientific Basis of 'Samadhi' – A Yogic Feat of Conditioning Human Body to a Specific Physiological State for Experiencing a Mentally 'Blissful' Condition: A Note for Critical Appraisal

"There is nothing that living things do that cannot be understood from the point of view, that they are made of atoms acting according to the laws of physics".

Richard P. Feynman (NL)

Introduction and background of universal reality

It is well known that the entire universe is full of only matter and energy. And this matter is made up of atoms to whom, we recognize as their elementary units. These atoms are available in only 118 different kinds and have been catalogued into the 'Periodic Table of Elements'. Atoms were first created in the nuclear furnaces of stars by fusion of the lightest atoms of hydrogen when the proverbial 'Big Bang' occurred. My own perception of this is that it just did not happen at one single point from where the matter spread to far distant places in the universe but such 'big-bang' like explosions must have happened simultaneously at thousands of locations within already existing space filled with dark energy. A rough calculation on the time required to travel for light at its velocity of (1,86,000 miles per second) from the farthest known distance in space observed by the Hubel Space Telescope to reach us, far more exceeds than the estimated (13.7 Billion years) life of the universe. It is still a mystery why and how the hydrogen protons as the first element came into being during the initial stage of formation of the universe. Particle accelerator experiments on smashing atoms, done at the European Centre for Nuclear Science (CERN) and at other institutions in the world have identified from the fragments of smashed atoms, the spectrum of elementary particles that constitute the composition of all matter. Still however, Scientists are far away from understanding the precise sequential order and how the quarks and other elementary particles themselves, the hydrogen protons and other elemental atoms first came into being. Hydrogen protons still constitute the most widely dispersed element in the entire universe. It has been estimated that only five percent of the universe is visible and the rest ninety five percent is invisible to human eye. This invisible matter has been named the dark matter or the dark energy.

Atoms constitute also the primary 'self-conscious (self-aware) material entities' because ever since their creation about 13.7 billion years ago, they have retained their individual identities and they all know as to who they are, what are their characteristics, capabilities, strengths and with which other atoms they can combine and in what proportions. When atoms of different elements combine together, they create compounded structures of various kinds, shapes *(Platonic crystal forms)* with varying characteristic physical and chemical properties. Such structural combinations have generally been classified as of mineral and polymorphic organic kinds, depending upon the predominance of other kinds of atoms over carbon chain molecules, respectively in their compositions. Molecules *(group of similar of dissimilar atoms bound together in a characteristic linear sequence or in a 3D configuration)* of both kinds i.e. purely mineral kinds and of the organic types have been observed to exist in the universe and on various objects such as meteorites, comets and planetary soils and their atmospheric environments. In view of these observations, it is generally believed that organic molecules that generate or that are specific to living objects are widely dispersed in the universe but these molecules, come into and assume forms, shapes, bodies with functions of various characteristic kinds under the influence of specific epigenetic *(Reference: Bruce Lipton)* and morphogenetic *(Reference: Rupert Sheldrake)* fields that exist specifically on a planet like the Earth. Such conditions for manifestation of living organisms have not been observed so far elsewhere in the visible universe, even through the eyes of the most powerful Hubble Space Telescope. We need to wait and see if the recently launched *(January 2022)* James Webb Space Telescope would be able to locate any kind of living organisms in the far deeper space, beyond the limits, the Hubble Space Telescope could see?

Current understanding on the structural organization of the universe and matter of which human and all life forms is an integral part

Human beings from their careful observations of the sky with the help of powerful telescopes, inter-planetary probes, satellites, developing clever theories, theoretical and computer simulation models and building very high energy particle accelerators and atom smashing machines have been able to reconstruct the events that happened when the actual 'big bang' occurred and thereafter through a time frame of first few seconds, minutes, days, years and centuries to the present time, with remarkable success. The cosmos we see today, exploded and expanded to almost its current size within first three minutes from a tiny speck of unimaginably high density dark matter at extremely high temperatures. The four fundamental forces- weak and strong interactions, electromagnetic and gravitation were all combined into a single unified force. Perhaps at the same time all the fundamental physical constants must have got dynamically tuned to their appropriate values for the universe to exist in its material form. It is believed that even minutest change in the values of physical constants would make it impossible for the universe to exist. Starting from the Planck epoch i.e. from 10^{-43} seconds to 10^{-36} seconds, the universe underwent a sudden, superfast, exponential expansion in a process known as the inflation with considerable drop in its initial temperature. Elementary particles appeared and protons and neutrons combined together, filling the universe with proto-elements, the precursors of the elements of matter. Quantum fluctuations during inflation stretched out to produce patterns which later determined the locations of galaxies. The universe became a hot, dense fireball, a gigantic accelerator of extremely high energies. The elementary particles we know today were born into it. Scientists think that several exotic particles of both matter and anti-matter types came first. They were followed by the more familiar and stabilized ones such as electrons, neutrinos and the quarks. The quarks soon combined to form the protons and neutrons which are collectively known as the baryons. Whereas the neutrinos escaped this plasma of charged particles to begin their uninterrupted travel through the expanding space, protons continued to remain trapped by the plasma. And when the universe cooled enough and violent collisions subsided, protons and neutrons somehow clubbed together to form the nuclei of light elements- hydrogen, helium and lithium in a process which has been specifically named as 'big bang nucleo-synthesis'. Protons are more stable than neutrons. Neutron decays with a half life of 15 minutes. As far as we know, protons may not decay at all. Still however in particle physics, proton decay is considered to be a hypothetical form of particle decay in which the proton decays into lighter subatomic particles such as a neutral pion and a positron. Therefore, protons will not decay into other particles on their own; because being the lightest and least energetic baryon. Many protons remained unpaired through the combinations and they make up about 74% of the mass of 'normal' matter found in the universe even today. Similarly, electrons have been found to be extremely stable particles in the universe. The life of electrons has been estimated to be 10^{66} years and this life-time is considerably more than the estimated life of the universe itself. Millenniums after the inflation began, the particle soup cooled down and electrons began to bind themselves to the positively charged nuclei to form electrically neutral atoms. This process is known by the term- recombination, wherein photons were set free to traverse uniformly through the length and breadth of the universe, forming a background of cosmic microwave radiation as remnants of the proverbial 'big bang' explosion and the cause of the matter–antimatter asymmetry.

It is the 'mighty electron' that drives the entire universe

Similar or dissimilar atoms combine together to form compounds by sharing or transfer of electrons from one atom to the others. So also, such compounds break apart when electrons are either prevented from or removed from the atoms. Therefore, it is the 'mighty electrons' that actually drive the entire universe and that includes both the inanimate and the animate matter. Hydrogen protons soon formed into a gas that filled the entire universe without emitting high energy photons. This situation prevailed for millions of years until a re-ionization process began with the formation of first stars with simultaneous release of highly energetic photons. These photons stripped electrons off from the neutral hydrogen atoms producing an infinite electric charge potential continuum across the universe. Matter began to form galaxies and clusters of galaxies with each galaxy containing over hundred billion stars. Our Sun, which is about 9.2 billion years old, is one of the 100 billion stars in our 'Milkyway galaxy'. It consists of mostly hydrogen and helium molecules produced by the fusion of hydrogen atoms and with release of thermal energy and electrically charged plasma. The universe today is still expanding and is maintaining a temperature of -270.42^0 degrees Celsius **(2.7 degrees Kelvin)**. The seventy percent of dark matter / dark energy present in the universe is believed to be driving the accelerated expansion of the universe as per the opinion of modern cosmologists. Does it automatically suggest that matter is created at the interface of the dark matter or the dark energy or the 'Black Hole? Cosmologists are of the view that 'Black Holes' are distributed throughout the universe. Is this also the reason why the universe is simultaneously expanding in all directions? Alternatively, does the so called *'Hiranyagarbha'* described in Sanskrit: हिरण्यगर्भः, literally meaning the 'golden womb' or a 'universal womb' is identifiable as the source of creation of the manifested material universe at the interface of the Black Holes or the Dark Energy? **'Hiranyagarbha'** finds mention in one hymn of the Rigveda (RV10.121), known as the **'Hiraṇyagarbha Sūkta'**. The widely accepted theory of 'Big-Bang' that happened about 13.8 billion years ago, resulted in the formation of the universe is also facing a serious challenge (see book by Eric Lerner) now.

Quark structure of 'matter'

Standard Model provides a unified description of the fundamental constituents of matter. Gell-Mann had shown that properties of all the particles that interact via the strong force can be understood if they were composed of quarks and anti-quarks. Quarks are bound together by the colour force to form particles such as protons, neutrons and pions that are collectively known as hadrons. These hadrons could no longer be considered as the elementary particles. Quarks form a deeper layer of matter from which all strongly interacting particles are formed. There are however another particles, such as the electron, that do not feel the strong force. Therefore electron cannot be composed of quarks. As far as anyone knows, the electron is a fundamental particle in its own right as it is not composed of any of more fundamental constituents. This puts the electron at par with the quarks as an elementary component of matter. A second particle that also does not feel the strong interaction is the neutrino. The neutrino is also considered to be elementary. There is yet another particle, which was detected in cosmic ray showers and is called the muon. The muon feels the electromagnetic and weak forces but not the strong force and muon is an exact replica of the electron in every respect except its mass. Whereas the mass of electron is 511 keV (0.511 MeV), the mass of muon is 105 MeV, making it just over two hundred times more massive and a heavy weight relative of the electron. And since muons do not feel the strong force and are not composed of quarks, muon is considered to be another fundamental particle without any substructure. In radioactive beta decay, the first manifestation of the weak force was discovered when along with an electron from an atomic nucleus, a neutrino was also detected. Similarly the production of muons is also accompanied by the emission of neutrinos. But the muon neutrino is not the same particle as the electron neutrinos. Electrons, muons and their associated neutrinos are collectively called as the leptons. This gives us two classes of matter particles: leptons and quarks. All matter is formed from leptons and quarks and that makes the great subdivision in the composition of matter. These particles are the modern equivalents of the atoms of chemical elements the ultimate building blocks of matter. Quarks feel the strong force whereas the leptons do not. However, both quarks and leptons feel the weak force. The weak force is responsible for the inter-conversion of a quark into another quark and a lepton into another lepton. But none of the known forces will convert a quark into lepton or a lepton into a quark.

A quick comprehensive review of the current understanding on the 'quark structure of matter' suggests that a total of just seven fundamental particles constitute visible matter and of these seven, four are leptons namely; electron, muon, electron neutrino and muon neutrino and three are the quarks namely; up quark, down quark and strange quark, together with their anti-particles. The small collection of these fundamental particles accounts for the structure of matter in a very neat and tidy way. Whereas, I consider all leptons and quarks to be merely particulate packets of quantized energy, the result of their combinations in building the atoms of various elements from the lightest hydrogen to the heaviest uranium, constitute the so called 'Conscious Entities'. Because, atoms of all the 118 known elements, ever since their creation 13.7 billion years ago, have not only retained their individual personal identities and integrities but they all know as to 'who' they are, what are their characteristics, capacities and have the knowledge and information about their proportional combining abilities with atoms of other elements to forge material structures of various kinds and characteristics. **Therefore, atoms constitute the primary 'conscious'**

'self-aware' material individuals in the universe. And all inanimate and animate matter existing in the universe is made from the combinations of two or more than two 'conscious atoms' of different elements. A question arises as to what is then an 'animate matter'? The primary unit of what we call the 'animate matter' is a 'biological CELL' and a cell itself is organized and built from the combinations of 'conscious atoms', the primary units of elements. Cell has acquired a special ability to sense the surrounding environment and communicate that information to the nucleus inside. Accordingly, the nucleus, with the help of the intervening medium (called the cytoplasm) that lies between the nucleus and the inner boundary wall of the cell, synthesize specific proteins to protect itself against the threats from the external environment to survive as an integral unit. The functions and actions of biological cells are fully automated electrically by exchange of electric charges and ionic currents, mediated across molecules and various membranes of organnels in sympathetic coordination with environment outside the cell wall. The primacy of all animate matter is the 'biological cell'. A cell may stay and survive as a singular unit *(unicellular bacteria)* or forge a callous of millions of other cells and organize themselves into an animated organism, with well defined functions for each specialized cell types to enable the organism to reproduce multiple copies of various cell types of their specific kinds and still survive against the forces of ever changing epigenetic environments. A biological cell therefore, is central to generating a conscious, self-aware organism. A question then arises; does the consciousness of a multi-cellular, multi-organ, organism represent a sum-total of collective consciousness of all individual 'conscious cells and all the atoms' that constitute it? And if the celebrated molecular *immuno*-pathologist, Candace B. Pert is to be believed, every cell of an organism constitutes its mind, the faculty that gives us our sense of experience of happiness, sorrow, excitement, depressions etc. and all sorts of facial grimaces. And all cells constituting an organism collectively enjoy or suffer the experience gained by an organism almost in unison. In short, the nature and amount of the proteins synthesized by cells induce changes in the physiology of the organism, sets its moods and temper and consequently the actions performed. The dynamic movements of the various organs (due to physical, biochemical or physiological action) of an organism, which is generally attributed to its free will, is in fact more due to the discharge of the electrical current *(ionic currents, in case* *of animate organisms)* within the various organs of the organism. This simple explanation cannot be easy to comprehend under the dogmatic influence, complexities and conscious or unconscious inheritance of our religious and philosophical beliefs for thousands of years, irrespective of communities of religious and social populations from anywhere on earth. An illustrative example of a practical dynamic movement, observed purely under the influence and flow of electrostatic or electric discharge, can be recalled from the observed fluttering of the American National Flag on the surface of the Moon, when Neil Armstrong installed it there on his landing. It is now well known that craters on the surface of Moon were also formed due to sudden discharges of static electricity at billions of volts, periodically built up on the moon surface. And the entire universe is now believed to be electrical in nature *(See extensive literature and videos from the Thunderbolts Project).* No surprise, well known scientists like Bruce Lipton and Robert Lanza are describing the universe essentially as 'bio-centric' and not 'material-centric' in nature as commonly believed. Inanimate material universe is of no philosophical consequence if there is no 'conscious observer' to appreciate and admire its infinite expanse, grandeur, complexities of creation, spectacular manifestations, sustenance and finally destruction over a period of time for cyclic self-regeneration. The faculty of **cognitive self-awareness** is therefore central to human understanding and comprehension of his relative position, power and limits in the scheme of universal creation.

Living organisms and their structural organization in general

Modern sciences of molecular biology, genetics, biochemistry, physiology and their related other sub-disciplines have emphatically proved that twenty different kinds of amino acids and the *DNA (di-oxy ribonucleic acid)* and RNA *(ribonucleic acid)* molecules form the fundamental basis for the generation, growth, sustenance and self-replication of all kinds of life-forms available on planet earth irrespective of their aquatic, terrestrial or atmospheric origins. The DNA forms part of the chromatin that constitutes the central nucleus of all biological cells. The nucleus is the central coordinating authority in dynamically organizing the synthesis of required specific proteins and other bio-molecules for protecting the cell for its survival against external epigenetic threats. At the same time, in the course of such dynamic adjustments, a continually on-going *intra-*

cellular process called the *DNA-methylation*, protects the integrity of the encoded DNA program of the organism. This fact makes it clear why survival strategies of all living organisms from the hottest Sahara to the coldest Arctic or Himalayan high altitude deserts are widely different. The *Vedic Sanatan* philosophy calls this way of living or situation-specific strategies for survival as the **'Dharma'**. Dharma is therefore, not a dogmatic, fanatic or a ritualistic tradition but a dynamically changing scientific strategy with logic, ethics and morality for healthful survival under given external or internal *(physiological)* situations. Regimented, dogmatic and fanatic enforcement of uniform functional rituals, taboos *(like sporting a long flowing beard without moustache to wearing particular kind and type of clothes and skull caps for men to wearing radiation and heat absorbing black coloured Robes and Hijabs for the poor women folks)*, restrictions, compulsions, forced convictions on adherents, are more akin to promoting a 'Robotic- Zombie Culture' by the operators of centrally controlled and organized politico-social pseudo-religions like Christianity and Islam. Such regimented taboos in the name of religions, have no comparison with the purely scientific *'Sanatan Vedic Dharma'*. I do not intend to suggest here that adherents of *Sanatan Vedic* Dharma are totally free of unscientific ritualistic practices. But they appear to have come into practice into society much later. And many of those are no longer observed by the people. To that extent, both the preachers and adherents of *Sanatan* Dharma are relatively more open to change with developments in science and technology. They are certainly not the captive slaves of the texts of their meta-narrative books that form the basis of the *'Sanatan* philosophy'. That is the reason, why there are innumerable critical commentaries written on almost all basic text books of the *Sanatan Vedic* Philosophy. This is certainly not true about the Bible and the Quran. I am sorry that the selfish politicians, crazy for vote-bank politics under the façade of running democracies, are gradually pushing the Sikhs in India also in the same mentality and mindset. Whereas, every piece of land in the world has been carved within framework of religious philosophies, only the Hindus in the world have been treacherously denied a nation under Hinduism even at the time of partition in 1947 on the basis of religion. Even Nepal, the only officially Hindu nation in the world has been pushed under the hold of barbaric Communist ideology by removing the monarchy in a sinister move. Heads of Christian Missionary Church are gradually realizing that without support from science and technology, preaching Christianity today will not be appealing and it is now difficult to attract the youth and to invoke them to surrender without reason and questions.

Innumerable examples of the celebrated Yogis from India since time immemorial and other Yoga-practitioners from elsewhere have demonstrated time and again how control over breathing and meditation protected them from the extremes of external epigenetic environmental fluctuations in enjoying a truly blissful condition mentally. **Mr. Wim Hof from the Netherlands in recent times has also demonstrated the power of controlled breathing and meditation to control the fluctuating mind and conditioning bodies by exposure to extreme cold temperatures and in conserving energy within for a truly blissful experience (e-Book-'The Wim Hof Method Explained' By Isabelle Hof, 2015, English Translation by Claire van den Bergh, Les Plus Belles, 2015. winhofmethod.com).** All this requires sincere regular practice, convictions, belief and determination on the part of a practitioner. Mr. Win Hof, who has developed and perfected his method- 'The Wim Hof Method', is now engaged in doing extensive experiments with professional scientists and collecting experimental data to put his method on modern scientific foundation. And his experiments involve in generating factual scientific parametric data on the effects of extreme cold baths and deep meditation and the physiological tuning of human bodies to experience 'Samadhi'-as a blissful condition of our mind. Mr. Wim Hof humbly says that what he has achieved is no supernatural power or magic but everyone can do it. So also the enlightened Mahatma Gautam Buddha (~500 BCE) during his own life time had clearly emphasized that he was neither God nor a messenger of a God. His enlightenment was not the result of a supernatural prowess, power, process or agency but rather the result of a close and minute attention he paid to the nature of the human mind which could be rediscovered by anyone for himself. How I wish, scientists in India should also initiate, promote and support such extensive scientific experiments in re-establishing the perennial relevance, importance and necessity of the *Sanatan* Vedic Yoga Practices for humanity. Mr. Wim Hof has listed a large number of benefits that are accrued from practicing deep meditation and exposure to extreme cold temperatures as are given below –

1. Helps to gain control over a range of physiological processes in the body even under extreme environmental and epigenetic conditions.

2. Enhanced intake of oxygen during deep breathing strongly affects biochemical and physiological activities of the body.
3. With deep breathing the diffusion surface area of the lungs where the exchange of Oxygen and Carbon dioxide takes place, increases from roughly 70 Sq meters to over 100 Sq meters, thereby increases the O_2 to CO_2 ratio to almost three times.
4. Enhances immunity of human body against infections from harmful bacteria several times than normal.
5. Exposure to extreme cold produces less 'cortisol' the stress hormone and also suppresses the inflammatory 'cytokines' that cause the flue like symptoms.
6. Meditation and deep breathing enhances the autonomic activities of the nervous system several times more than the normal.
7. Exposure to extreme cold temperatures, reduce the levels of several inflammatory proteins to almost zero and leads to an increase in the number of white blood cells, which combat emergence of any diseases.
8. Regular Cold Baths enhance the brown fat levels within body which produce more heat in the body than white fat that merely stores energy.

In 2013, a 53 year old Sri Lankan Buddhist practitioner of *Samadhi* was subjected to both fMRI and EEG to observe the status of his brain during progressive stages of the *Samadhi Yog* by a group of researchers. They observed a decrease in parietal lobe activation which is involved in receiving sensory information to determine the special orientation of the body and where the self is located in the space. The flow of blood to this area was observed to decrease with progressive stages of the Samadhi. Apparently, this supports the notion from neuro-scientific point of view that experiencing a sense of unity with the surrounding epigenetic environment is a part of the enlightened experience during Samadhi. Additionally, both Broca's and Wernicke's areas in the brain are progressively deactivated with the progress of Samadhi. Since both these areas of brain are involved in production and comprehension of language, the observation suggests that the path to Samadhi involves the sensation of some kind of internal dialogue and linguistic thoughts. In view of the subjective nature of the experience during Samadhi, no ancient texts or spiritual Guru can analytically explain in spoken or written words what this experience factually is. At the same time, due to purely personal nature of spiritual experiences, it can be very difficult to trust even a so called enlightened person that there is such an experience. This is where objective science becomes very useful in that it helps to physically measure and gather all physical, physiological and biometric parameters of a practitioner of Samadhi and prove that these parameters do indeed change in Samadhi. Under such a state of change, the characteristic experiences of mindfulness or bliss gained by practitioners of Samadhi in general appear to be similar if not equally identical. Still however, it is almost certain that experience of bliss is indeed a product and result of willfully altered physiology of human body and synthesis of specific hormones and proteins in the body system through practice of controlled breathing, concentration of thought and meditation.

References

1. 'Molecules of Emotion: Everything you need to know to feel Go(o) d. The Science Behind Mind–Body–Medicine' Candace B. Pert, Simon and Schuster, 1999.

2. 'The Electric Universe' Wallace Thornhill and David Talbot, Mikamar Publishing, 2007.

3. 'The Thunderbolts Project' The Official Website of 'The Thunderbolts Project™'.

4. 'The Biology of Belief: Unleashing the Power of Consciousness, Matter and Miracles' Bruce H. Lipton, Hay House, India, 2015.

5. 'Biocentrism' Robert H. Lanza and Bob Berman, Ben Bella Books, 2010.

CHAPTER – 5

A Search for the Scientific Meaning and Basis to the *'Puranic'* Story of *'Samudra-Manthan'* i.e. Churning of the 'Cosmic Ocean' by the 'Devas' and the 'Asuras': An Attempted Synthesis

Abstract

This article attempts to describe and discuss the ancient concept of *'Samudra Manthan'*, the proverbial churning of the cosmic ocean by the *Devatas* (the Gods) and the *Asuras* (the Devils) from the Puranas, in the light of the modern theories on the origin of universe. It should not be considered as a 'WILD GUESS' by the author but a sincere and logical interpretation and attempt in decoding of the story from the point of view of modern scientific knowledge. It must be remembered that the *Devatas* and the *Asuras* are the symbolic personified representations of the emerging forces of nature during and after the formation of the universe. In the light of these, the author has identified the *Devatas* as the personified representations for the material particles that originated in the 'Big Bang' and so also the *Asuras* to be the personified representation of the 'Antimatter' that originated simultaneously. As long as the amount of matter and antimatter produced, balanced each other, there was no beginning for the formation of the manifested material universe. But as the amount of antimatter decreased / vanished, the amount of visible matter and its accumulation into formation of the universe began. The antimatter that anihillated all matter produced, has been logically identified to be the ancient *Puranic*- deadly poison described as the proverbial-*'Halahal'* consummed by Lord Shiva and saved both the Asuras and the Devatas from almost certain annihilation and destruction. It therefore appears that the so called 'Halahal' which Lord Shiva drank, must have been the kind of a mysterious destructive force, that was killing the matter and antimatter alike, involved in the primordial conversion of the dark matter / dark energy into visible proto- matter. In another suggestive and innovative analogy, following his discussion on the fourteen jewels that emerged from the churning of the cosmic ocean, the author has ventured to not only logically identify those fourteen jewels but also the so called 'Five Pranas' *(Panch Pranas)*. The author argues that the prototype of the self-replicating DNA and RNA molecules must have found their assemblage after the space along with its contents began to settle down and rearrange into stable configuration with least entropy.

Figure 1. *'Samudra Manthan': Picture credit: Pintrest website, free Downloads*

Introduction and perennially descending story of *samudra manthan*

The *Samudra* (Ocean) *Manthan* (Churning) is a very important supposedly historical episode about the cosmological evolution of the universe described in the 'Sanatan Philosophical' literature the *'Puranas'*. The churning of the milky ocean, in search of the proverbial 'A*amrut'* (Nectar elixir), took place and during this churning, 14 different Jewels *(Ratnaas)* emerged from the proverbial cosmic ocean along with the 'Amrut'. Thirteen of these 14 jewels (Ratnaas) were divided among the *Devas* and the *Asuras*, however, there were no takers for the 14th jewel (Ratnaa) the *'Halahal'*, which was known to be the deadliest poison and which could destroy everything that came into being with the universe. Neither the *Devas* nor the *Asuras* wanted such a deadly poison. But it had to be somehow given to either of them. Since nobody was coming forward, Lord Shiva drank this poison and stored that in his throat and saved both the *Devas* and the *Asuras* from almost certain destruction / annihilation / extinction.

This story is not an ordinary description for amusement as a folklore but to me, it represents a link / or a clue in a descriptive coded language for a sequential understanding about what must have physically happened during the first few seconds or minutes when the universe came into being from the most condensed form of pure energy *(dark matter or dark energy)* into a material form. Today, we recognize this event by the name of 'Big Bang'. Cosmologists and astrophysicists tell that only 5% of the material universe is visible to us and rest 95% is invisible. This invisible universe is believed to be made of 'Dark Matter' or 'Dark Energy'. Its presence is detected only by means of the gravitational force and not by any other means. The nature, composition, and conditions of existence and extent of dark matter are only a matter of wild speculation despite tremendous advancement in science of cosmology, elementary particle physics and astrophysics.

To me, the story of '*Samudra Manthan*' is certainly connected to the condition and origin of the early universe, the initial turmoil and its dynamic readjustment under various types of emerging forces, energies and forms of active proto-elemental matter which came into being, their combinations and onset of the process of stabilization to acquire the least entropy configuration.

In the '*Sanatan Vedic Philosophy*', all natural forces of various kinds have been visualized, symbolized and described as the specifically personified *Deva / Devata* with well-defined attributes and functions. Therefore the various terms that appear in the Puranic story of *Samudra Manthan* need to be first decoded and then correlated with possible corresponding equivalent modern scientific terms, before joining the dotted lines for a truly comprehensive understanding of the story, on the logic of modern scientific theories and developments in cosmology. I find it, as a challenging opportunity and hopefully, should be able to do so, at least in a small measure, in the following description. It may be noted that the status of the universe today, is practically no different from what it was at the time of the Vedic and Puranic times, when the visualization and description about the '*Samudra Manthan*' was first conceived, conceptually crystallized, attempted to be understood and logically narrated. And this time frame is believed to be roughly 25,000 years BC or possibly even more (Reference Dr. P. V. Vartak).

Let us now go logically to identify and decode the individual Deva / Devata and other terms for near corresponding equivalent from the modern scientific theories on cosmology. I would request my learned readers to be open to the following ideas without dogmatic faith / belief / or prejudice in whatever exists already at the back of their mind since childhood, previous readings, study, faith, beliefs or perceptions.

What is meant by 'samudra' and it's 'manthan' in the puranic story?

The word 'samudra' meaning the ocean in the story should not be confused with something we find on the Earth filled with water. As I understand the term, this 'samudra' refers to the infinite entity of pure energy (Dark energy?) that must have existed before the visible universe came into being. And that is the cosmic electrostatic continuum of electric charge in the form of densely packed hydrogen atoms (Protons) as the starting point. And this state of the universe must have happened long after the proverbial 'Big Bang' actually occurred. This is because very early universe would not have had any visible matter whatsoever except an infinite, uniform, densely packed, continuum of energy. The sequential story of what triggered and happened in the formation of early universe within first few seconds or minutes from the 'Big Bang' is still not very clear. It is still a matter of speculation and wild logical guess because the very science of material atomic elements was at its beginning. The sequential events until the emergence of hydrogen protons in the early universe is a mixture of some very complex and intriguing incidences, which are yet to be grasped by modern science. But, what we understand from the current 'Stellar Chemistry' being, that atoms of heavier atomic weight were built up from the fusion of hydrogen atoms under the conditions of extremely high temperatures and pressures that existed at that time. And we have seen now from the monumental work of Albert Einstein- the special theory of relativity and his famous equation $E= mC^2$ indicating that matter and energy are interchangeable. The newly formed elemental atoms, forged newer combinations with each other and created structures of huge cosmic dimensions which we observe in the sky. Here, the physical emergence and the role of electrons or the electric charge per say, in the formation of material structures, must have already got defined by now. And because all these, huge structures came into being from a vast invisible ocean of pure energy, like the 'butter' that coagulates and float out as a result of the churning of the butter milk, the ancient Sages must have used the term-'Manthan- meaning churning' in describing the origin of the universe and the process of churning of the cosmic ocean of pure energy as the 'Samudra Manthan'.

Who are the devas / devata?

Most possibly *'Devas'* represent the primordial matter that came into being and had the capacity for independent existence as (starting from the Quarks, Electrons, Protons, Neutrons and Neutrino) and elemental Hydrogen atoms and their fusion together to produce larger atoms of different elements of higher atomic weights. Hydrogen is the primary and most dominant component of the all pervading electric plasma (within and in-between millions and millions of interconnected clusters of galaxies) in the universe even today.

Who are the asuras / daityaas?

Most possibly, *'Asura'* must be broadly representing the 'antimatter' in the universe. For every kind of material particle there was a simultaneous creation of its anti-material particle. As long as the amount of that primordial matter and antimatter was produced in balanced quantities in the universe, or perhaps antimatter was in dominant condition, there was no beginning to the formation of the visible 'universe'. Somehow, when the amount of antimatter of the kind of *'Halahaal' which was preventing the formation of matter,* started diminishing by a hitherto unknown and un-identified process of their destruction or annihilation, the physical accumulation of matter began with simultaneous expansion of the space. The 'Force', that individually or in consonant combination with other forces, diminished or annihilated the antimatter from the universe was most likely personified and named as the 'Shiva'. And the antimatter, the deadly poison, which was preventing matter from coming into existence until it was consumed by the personified *Deity called* 'Shiva' to be the proverbial poison- the 'Halahaal'. Matter began accumulating in the universe only after the amount of antimatter was diminished or totally destroyed. The duel between the forces, producing matter and antimatter or between the proverbial *Devas* and *Asuras* in the formation of the material universe- is what appears to be the proverbial *'Samudra Manthan'*. A question arises, if this *samudra manthan* was an isolated one-time incidence that happened, after the beginning of the formation of universe and the 'Big Bang' occurred? Perhaps not. The process may be continually going on ever since, at far lower levels of energies than at the start. Since greater amount of force / energy is required to first initiate an action in any system than to sustain it for continued long durations. Dan Hooper, in his well-known book-*'At the Edge of Time'* has described the process in a lucid way as follows;

"Even the origin of "ordinary" matter harbors stubborn secrets of its own. Although protons, neutrons, and electrons, and the atoms they constitute, can be easily created through well-understood processes, such processes also create an equal quantity of more exotic particles, known as antimatter. Whenever particles of matter and antimatter are brought into contact with one another, both are annihilated. So why, then, does our universe contain so much matter and so little antimatter? In fact, why is there any matter at all? If matter and antimatter had been created in equal amounts in the heat of the Big Bang- as our current understanding of physics would lead us to expect-then almost all of it would have been destroyed long ago, leaving our universe essentially devoid of atoms. Yet, there are atoms all around us. Somehow, more matter than antimatter must have been created in the first fraction of a second of our universe's history. We do not know how or when this came to pass, or what mechanism was responsible. But somehow, something about the conditions of the early universe made it possible for the seeds of atoms- and all of chemistry, including life-generating- molecular assemblies of atoms, to survive the heat of the Big Bang. It is also intriguing; when and how the various 'universal physical constants' came to evolve, stabilized and fixed their appropriate values during the on-going dynamic process of evolution of the universe?

Going back even further in time, we come to what is perhaps most intriguing of our cosmic mysteries. In order to make sense of our universe as we observe it, cosmologists have been forced to conclude that space, during its earliest moments, must have undergone a brief period of hyper-fast expansion. Although this epoch of inflation, lasted only a little longer than a millionth of a billionth of a billionth of a billionth of a second, it left our universe utterly transformed. In many ways, one can think of the end of inflation as the true beginning of the universe that we live in. Despite identifying the many compelling reasons to think that inflation really took place, cosmologists do not understand about this early, key era of our cosmic history".

What is the known and widely accepted structure of the universe today?

There are four fundamental forces of nature identified by physicists as gravitation, electromagnetism, strong and weak nuclear interactions. These four forces interact with each other and those interactions generate fields which in turn interact to produce all the observable material phenomena of the universe. Some people think that those four fundamental forces should be able to be unified since they do interact, indicating that they share an underlying interact-able principle. One principle they share is the measurement of their forces, called "energy" in physics. Energy is a measure of force; it is not an object or a structure. But it is that thing, which is a common constituent of everything that exists; and it means that either it exerts some force or it does not exist.

In practical terms, the word "universe" refers to an idea, the sum of all things that materially and visibly exists. It is not an object and does not have a structure. The closest thing to a structure that would relate all things that exist (the "universe") is the set of so-called "laws" or first principles regarding how those four fundamental forces come into manifestation and interaction. For example, the principle of least action which informs us that it takes more energy to start something than to keep it going; the 1st "law" of thermodynamics which informs us that energy can neither be created nor be destroyed, a principle which makes origin narratives moot; entropy, the tendency for heat energy to become evenly distributed over time in a closed, isolated system, special relativity which informs us that there can be no privileged location anywhere (no center therefore no geometric structure nor time frame, no beginning, no ending). The evolution and 'fine tuning' of the values of fundamental 'universal physical constants' form an integral prelude to the process of evolution of the universe. A minutest change in the values of these physical constants would have made the origin and sustained existence of the universe almost impossible.

When it comes to its composition that can be looked up? The most common form of matter is the atomic elemental Hydrogen, by far. All other versions of the matter are made in stars by fusion of this Hydrogen into heavier atomic elements. Then there are all the fields and their quantum excitations; for information about that, refer to the Standard Model of "particle" (quantum excitations of the fields) physics. We should look at both the periodic table of elements and the spectrum of electromagnetic energies (radiant energy, photons).

One more "map" of reality that must pique our interest: the musical scale with only seven notes and the visible light with only seven coloured hues. Yes, the musical scale, because all forms of energy oscillate and oscillations are all on a scale of frequencies with associated wavelengths. For that matter, the musical scale is a kind of structural map for the oscillations, a fundamental feature of our universal physical reality. And to me, this musical scale extends from the subtlest 'quarks' to gamma rays, x-rays, ultra-violet, visible, infrared, microwaves, radio waves and further beyond into inter stellar and inter-galactic 'Kristian Berkland Electric Current' wavelengths and frequencies. Here, I would like to mention the work of Joel Sternheimer in France on vibrating frequencies of protein crystals and their corresponding musical notes and their effects on the induced growth and early maturity of plants, indicating a possible clue in such a connection. The identification of seven energy grid-centers, with characteristic frequencies, within every human body, known as the 'Chakras' is another mysteriously perceived and experienced reality. These seven 'Chakras' are known to not only control the functioning of various organs that constitute a human body as an integrated individual organism but also to regulate and maintain the connection and circulation of universal cosmic electric potential energy (Cosmic Universal Consciousness) within the body system as an integral part of the universe.

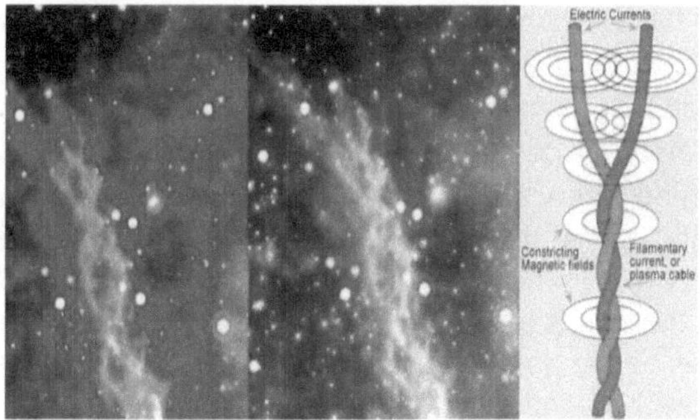

Figure 2. Factual photograph of the coiled Kristian Birkland currents in space

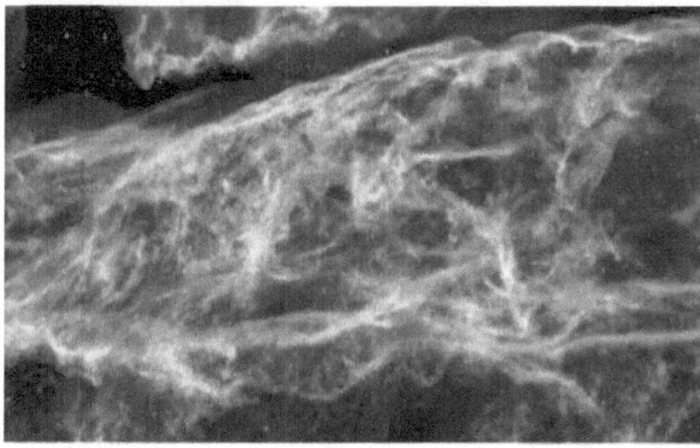

Figure 3. 'Kristian Birkland' Nebulae photographed in Space *(source: Google)*

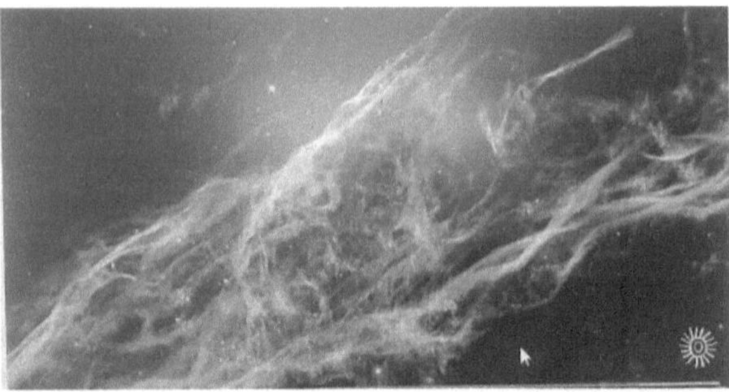

Figure 4. Here is a photograph of the twisted strands and braids of 'Kristian Birkland' electric Currents as photographed by the James Web Space Telescope recently. (*Reproduced with apologies as a screen shot from the video: Twisted Pairs and Braids Everywhere by Wallace Thornhill-Thunderbolts*)

The origins of everything: the quark structure of 'matter'

Cosmologists have discovered that most of the energy in the universe is available in the form of what is popularly known as dark matter and dark energy. We can neither touch dark matter nor see dark energy in a direct way. We are also not perceived to be made directly of these mysterious materials. Instead, everything in the universe experienced by us is made of atoms and only atoms, the basic building blocks of matter. The study of atoms generally falls in the realm of chemistry, wherein, chemists study and describe how the atoms behave and bind with atoms of other elements to form molecules of compounds. The Cosmologists on the other hand, study atoms to unravel how these atoms actually got formed and came into being for independent existence with characteristic individual identities. Further, there are more perplexing questions about how and why quarks and electrons, the fundamental constituents of all atoms on their part –came into being. The subject of cosmology has advanced so much now that we can easily calculate how many quarks were initially present in the initial stage of the early universe and how their quantity changed as our universe expanded and cooled. We can also estimate when these quarks coalesced in groups of three, to form the first protons and neutrons. However, in-depth calculations done, suggest that very few quarks and very few electrons should have survived beyond first few seconds after the Big Bang and the universe should have been practically free of atoms. But the fact that the universe is full of a large number of atoms (of 118 different kinds) is a proof of the inadequacy of our understanding. Apparently, there is something amiss. Our universe must have contained some 'mysterious kind of force or matter or energy' during the first fraction of a second from the Big Bang that we have never observed in any experiments involving giant atom smashing machines. This 'mysterious force or matter or energy' must have been the cause of significant transformative events, soon after the Big Bang, such as the sudden annihilation of antimatter. And we still do not know anything about it. What we know for certain being that this fact is true and we would not exist if it were not.

Using giant atom smashing machines, physicists have learnt that our young and hot universe was initially filled with a soup, containing not only the known kind of particles of matter; quarks, electrons, protons, neutrons and neutrinos but also their antiparticles; antiquarks, positrons, antiprotons, antineutrons and antineutrinos. No matter is created without creating an equal amount of its antimatter. And whenever any matter is destroyed, its antimatter is also destroyed simultaneously along with it. Matter and antimatter are created and destroyed in conjunction with each other. And if this is really so, then we have to ask ourselves: How did we come to be living in a universe that is filled with so much of matter, while containing so little or practically no antimatter at all? Where did all of the antimatter go? And why did not all the matter go with it?

According to what we know about our universe and its physical laws, all kinds of matter-antimatter pairs should have been destroyed far more often than new pairs were created and the universe would have been totally free of any matter. And yet we observe that matter exists in the universe. Somehow, some kind of an unknown mechanism, process or event--- must have stepped in to prevent destruction of matter with either reduction or removal of the antimatter *(a destructive poison for matter)*. To be more precise, something must have happened in the primordial soup formed after the Big Bang that caused an imbalance in the amount of matter present to become slightly greater than the amount of antimatter. It is only because of this primordial asymmetry, a small but significant amount of matter has survived in the universe. Physicists are still trying to work out how this small imbalance between matter and antimatter came about? And this fact gives us an important hint. Some mysterious kind of particles must have been present or events happened during the first fraction of a second after the Big Bang. But for this unknown and mysterious possibility, there would have been no atoms, no gas, no dust, no stars, no galaxies, no planets and no life. Has that 'mysterious matter and energy' some connection with the proverbial poison 'Halahaal' which the personified Lord Shiva in the *Puranic* story on *'Samudra Manthan'* drank to save the universe from annihilation?

Standard Model provides a unified description of the fundamental constituents of matter. Gell-Mann had shown that properties of all the particles that interact via the strong force can be understood if they were composed of quarks and antiquarks. Quarks are bound together by the colour force to form particles such as protons, neutrons and pions, which are collectively known as hadrons. These hadrons could no longer be considered as the elementary particles. Quarks form a deeper layer of matter from which all particles interacting strongly with each others are formed. However, there are particles, such as the electron, that do not feel the strong force. Therefore, electron cannot be composed of quarks. As far as anyone knows, the electron is a fundamental particle in its own right as it is not composed of any of more fundamental constituents. This puts the electron at par with the quarks as an elementary component of matter. A second particle that also does not feel the strong interaction is the neutrino. The neutrino is also considered to be elementary. There is yet another particle, which was detected in cosmic ray showers and is called the muon. The muon feels the electromagnetic and weak forces but not the strong force and muon is an exact replica of the electron in every respect except its mass. Whereas the mass of electron is 511 keV (0.511 MeV), the mass of muon is 105 MeV, making it just over two hundred times more massive and a heavy weight relative of the electron. And since muons do not feel the strong force and are not composed of quarks, muon is another fundamental particle without any substructure. In radioactive beta decay, the first manifestation of the weak force was discovered when along with an electron from an atomic nucleus, a neutrino was also detected. Similarly the production of muons is also accompanied by the emission of neutrinos. But the 'muon neutrino' is not the same particle as the 'electron neutrinos'. Electrons, muons and their associated neutrinos are collectively called as the leptons. This gives us two classes of matter particles: leptons and quarks. All matter is formed from leptons and quarks and that makes the great subdivision in the composition of matter. These particles are the modern equivalents of the chemical elements the ultimate building blocks of matter. Quarks feel the strong force whereas the leptons do not. However, both quarks and leptons feel the weak force. The weak interaction force is responsible for the inter-conversion of a quark into another quark and a lepton into another lepton. But none of the known forces convert a quark into a lepton or a lepton into a quark.

A quick glance at the current scenario suggests that a total of just seven fundamental particles constitute matter and of these seven, four are leptons namely; electron, muon, electron neutrino and muon neutrino and three quarks namely; up, down and strange together with their corresponding antiparticles. The small collection of these fundamental particles accounts for the structure of matter in a very neat and tidy way.

Super-symmetry in nature

Fundamental particles have been classified into two separate classes that display completely different behavior. One class of particles form-the constituents of matter, while the other class of particles mediate the forces that hold this matter together. Matter forming particles such as the electron obey the Wolfgang Pauli's exclusion principle, which means that each one of these must exist in a different wave state. And this curious property is shared by all the fundamental particles from which matter is formed and they include; protons, neutrons and the quarks. In fact it is this property that enables them to condense into matter and collectively they are known as fermions after Italian physicist Professor Enrico Fermi. Likewise, the particles whose exchange produces a force, such as photons behave in a completely different way because they exist in the same wave state and form a single wave (e.g. Laser). Particles that behave in this way are collectively known as bosons after the Indian physicist Professor Satyendra Nath Bose. The matter and the force-carrying particles could then be paired up, with force-carrying particle for each matter particle and *vice versa*. This is the sort of a deep relationship that is believed to be lying at the heart of matter and that is what the physicists are exactly striving for to unravel. A unity, that leads to more profound understanding of the universe. Its discovery would represent a major step forward towards total unification of all the four forces of nature and all the particles within a single theory to which the name – 'Super-symmetry' has been given. Super-symmetry has therefore been described as- 'a symmetry between matter-forming particles and force-mediating particles. And 'Super-symmetry' is believed to unite the matter and force particles together in a warm, mutual metaphorically masculine embrace of the sturdy mass particles entwined with the metaphorically feminine force-carrying particles. Now compare and contrast this scientific fact to the ancient *Sanatan Vedic* philosophy of always pairing masculine– Bramha, Vishnu and Mahesh with their feminine counterparts Saraswati, Lakshmi and Parvati respectively. Further, the theoretical demand of 'super-symmetry' requiring matter-carrying particles and force-carrying particles to essentially have equal amount of electric charge on them for pairing is akin to the concept of 'Ardha-Nari-Nateshwara' equal halves of masculine Shiva and feminine Parvati in the constitution of human body (See the figure given below).

Figure 5. *As a composite of equal halves of masculine Shiva (left) and feminine Parvati (right), most possibly, the ancient Sanatan Vedic concept of 'Artdha-Nari-Nateshwar' is a symbolic representation of the existence of 'Super-symmetry' in nature, now predicted by the modern 'Standard Model of Particle Physics'. For that matter, masculine Bramha and feminine Saraswati, masculine Vishnu and feminine Lakshmi represent the other two 'super-symmetric' forces of nature.*

If the universe is really governed by the super-symmetric laws, then it is expected that each type of matter-carrying particle must have its complementary super-symmetry force-mediating partner. Conversely, each force-mediating particle have its super-symmetric matter-carrying particle. Theoretically matter-carrying particle and force-carrying particles for super-symmetry pairing must have exactly the same amount of electric charges, but this is not the case for the particles that are currently known to physicists, therefore all the known particles cannot be paired up in this way. Therefore, if super-symmetry is indeed the symmetry of the real world, then it would imply the existence of many different new particles to be discovered in the years to come. There would be a new super-partner particle for each of the known particle. And physicists, in anticipation of their discovery in the years to come, have already provided suitable names for all such particles. Their suggested names for instance being; super-partner of photon will be known as photino, super-partners of W and Z particles will be known as Winos and Zinos, super-partner of gluon as gluinos, super-partner of Higgs is Higgsino and that of electron and quark as selectron and squark respectively. Their discovery would reveal the origin of the dark matter so abundantly distributed in the universe.

What is the classical view of 'matter'?

Anything that occupies space and has mass is called as matter. Matter is generally found in three states; solid, liquid and gases at normal temperature and pressure and in the fourth state called the plasma at extremely high temperatures. All matter is made up of atoms, the smallest building blocks of elements. As on today, there are only 118 different kinds of elements in the universe and they have been classified into the Periodic Table of elements. Atoms are themselves built from three fundamental particles called the protons, neutrons and the electrons. Protons and neutrons stay inside the central core of all atoms called the nucleus and the electrons revolve round the nucleus in regular orbits. Protons carry positive electric charge, electrons carry negative electric charge whereas neutrons are electrically neutral. This makes central nuclei of all atoms to be electrically positive. The total positive charge due to protons in all atoms is equal to the total negative charge due to electrons and all atoms therefore always remain electrically neutral.

How does the elemental atomic matter interact together?

All basic books on chemistry tell us that atoms of various kinds available in the universe combine together according to their combining capacity described by their 'valency'. Further refinement of our understanding revealed that the combinations of atoms in forging newer structures of various kinds is governed by either sharing in common or donating one or more of the 'valency electrons' from the outermost electron orbits of one atom to the other. Thereby, forming electrovalent or the covalent kind of bonds between the two combining atoms. The atom that donates its electrons to another atom assumes a net positive charge and is called a positive anion. The atom that receives electrons from its donor, assumes a net negative charge and is called a negative cation. The bond strength of the combination depends upon the number of electrons donated or shared between the combining atoms and reflects on the stability of the structures that come into being from such combinations. Higher the bond strength, higher will be the requirement of energy to break those bonds. Protein molecules involving nitrogen atoms are known to forge such stable structures and decades or hundreds of years pass before they break down under normal conditions.

How does the matter get destroyed?

Obviously, structures forged between atoms of various kinds, break down when external energy in amount more than the bond strengths is supplied to the structure. Atoms can also be separated from their combinations when a medium with very high capacity to hold electric charges separately within itself, such as water with high dielectric constant intervenes in between. To sum up, it is the electrons that forge combinations between atoms of similar or dissimilar kinds. It is electrons that destroy the combinations between various atoms under various incompatible situations. Electrons are universally present everywhere and are known to be indestructible and most stable of all known elementary particles. The life of electrons has been estimated to be 10^{66} Years, a life span which is more than the estimated life of the universe itself. Electrons are the common constituents of all atoms and form a universal electric potential continuum. This universal electric potential continuum has been identified by Moharir (Ref.3) to be the 'universal consciousness / universal Soul' of which, the entire material and living organisms form an integral part. No surprise, James Morgia (Ref.4) in his celebrated book, emphatically declares that it is "the mighty electron that recycles all in the entire universe."

One-electron universe

Celebrated physicist John Wheeler in spring of the year 1940, proposed his postulate of –'One-electron universe' during his telephonic conversation with Richard Feynman. According to this hypothesis, all electrons and positrons are actually manifestations of a single entity moving backwards and forwards in time. All electrons have the same mass and same charge because according to Wheeler– "Because, they are all the same electron!". John Wheeler based his idea on the world lines traced out across space-time by every electron. Rather than having myriad such lines, they could all be parts of one single line like a huge tangled knot traced out by the one-electron. Any given moment of time during movement of electron in a tangled knot, is represented by a slice across space-time. And this slice would meet the knotted line trace of the electron a great number of times. Every such meeting point indeed represents a real electron at that moment. At those points of intersections, half the lines will be directed forward in time and other half looped around in the backward direction. Wheeler suggested that all electrons at the backward sections would appear to electrons in the forward directions as their antiparticles i.e. positrons. And positrons could simply be represented as electrons going from future to the past in a back section of their world lines according to Richard Feynman. Not only are all electrons the same electron, but all positrons, the antimatter component of electrons are also the same electrons moving backwards. Yoichiro Nambu (Ref.5) applied it later to all production and annihilation of particles-antiparticle pairs, describing the 'eventual creation and annihilation of pairs that may sporadically occur every now and then, is factually neither a creation nor an annihilation, but only a change of directions of moving particles from past to future or *vice versa*. Incidentally, it implies, that at any given instant of time, an equal number of electrons would appear to be created and simultaneously annihilated with no matter in balance. Although, the concept of 'one-electron universe' has not been backed up by experimental evidence so far, there is merit in the logical arguments supporting it. I personally foresee a universal electric potential continuum Or a universal cosmic consciousness as a factual realty of which every living and non-living matter is an integral part (Ref. 3).

A word about the description of the other jewels 'ratnaas' that emerged from the *'samudra manthan'*

The proverbial *'samudra manthan'* has been described to have produced 14 invaluable 'Ratnaas' / Jewels as a result of the churning of the ocean of electrostatic potential energy continuum–'the samudra'. And these fourteen jewels have been described to be (1) Lakshmi- the feminine consort of Vishnu (2) Kaustubh Jewel –worn by Lord Vishnu (3) Kalpa Vruksha- the wish fulfilling tree of Parijaat producing never fading blossom of flowers (4) Sura or Varuni –the wines or alcohols (5) Dhanvantaari- the divine physician of the Devatas (6) Chandra-the Moon, the satellite or most likely a configurative pattern of all the energy producing stars with their satellite moon (s) as a balanced structure for the evolution of the universe (7) Kamadhenu-wish granting cow (8) Airavata- the white elephant (9) Rambha- the feminine angles (10) Uchhaishvara –the seven headed horse which most probably represents the first emergence of the electromagnetic energy, now known to be the visible spectrum to human eye (11) Halahaal the deadly poison (12) Hari Dhanu- the Sharanga Bow (13) The Shankha-the Counch and finally (14) the Amrut-the immortalizing liquid Nectar. As I personally visualize the scenario described, the appearance of all these fourteen jewels, only represent the formation of molecular assemblies into some kind of the blueprints of basic formative stabilized structure or configuration with potential to coming into their definite physical form, shape, morphology and self-generating, self-assembled, self-replicating, self-sustaining morphogenetic individuals as products of congenial epigenetic conditions, such as on the Earth and possibly anywhere in the space-time geometry. A recent evidence to substantiate this argument comes from the identification of 20 amino acids, the building blocks of all life, from the rock samples of asteroid 'Ryugu' which is more than 200 million miles (320 million kilometers) from Earth. These asteroid rock samples were drilled, collected and retrieved back on Earth by the Japanese (JAXA) Hayabusa 2 spacecraft, that landed on the asteroid in 2018 and was launched by the Japanese Aerospace Exploration Agency (Science Alert, Today's Top News, June 10, 2022). Another study conducted on a 3.3 billion years old rock discovered in South Africa (Geochimica et Cosmochimica Acta, 2019) also indicates the possibility that some- if not all- of these life-building molecules first came to Earth on comets and asteroids. The Ryugu findings make the evidence that asteroids carry these molecules even much stronger.

What are the likely 'panch praan'?

In this context, the assembly of the primordial protein and other organic molecules and particularly the self-replicating Deoxyribonucleic acid (DNA) and the Ribonucleic acid (RNA) appear to be significantly important.

It is quite likely, that the molecular DNA or the RNA template blueprints of all the fourteen *'Ratna's'* that emerged from the early formative universe and described in the ancient story of *Samudra Manthan*, were factually assembled during this time. These DNA and RNA molecules in their turn assembled together and formed characteristic organisms from unicellular to multi-cellular organs and organisms with an inbuilt machinery and mechanism for their self-reproduction, when congenial epigenetic and morphogenetic environment as available on Earth was found. For that matter, I seriously consider that the five essential bio-molecular component assemblies of (1) Adenine (2) Thymine (3) Cytosine and (4) Guanine, called as the 'Bases' of DNA molecules and (5) Uracil in the RNA molecules but absent in the DNA, with definitive programs for synthesis of specific proteins, may indeed be constituting the so called –*'Panch Praan'* (the five Praan) that create, sustain and move all the biological organisms. All biologically living organisms are known to evolve, exist, sustained, function because of specific proteins and their synthesis within individual body systems.

The concept of 'Praan' has been mentioned, described and discussed, since time immemorial in respect of only the living creatures as the primary force behind their existence. And since the concepts of the five 'Praan' have been in existence in the minds of human psyche since time immemorial, there must be some seat for their residing and operation within body systems of living organisms in general and within human body in particular. And perhaps, the DNA and RNA molecules appear to be the only possible locations where these five 'praan' may be residing. The five base pairs; Adenine, Thymine, Cytosine, Guanine and Uracil, in various sequential combinations are triggered into action by the external epigenetic and morphogenetic environment, for synthesizing various proteins for perpetual working of bio-molecular factory and for organization and working of self- sustaining, self-replicating organisms under continual stimulus and control of the universal electric charge. Based upon their specific functions involved in the working of all organisms, but specifically in relation to the working of a human body, these five Praana, have been described in Vedic literature as– *Praan, Apaan, Samaan, Udaan and Vyaan*. Whereas, the primary universal electric charge that motivates the five Pranaas to subject the DNA molecules into action, represents the 'Maha-praana or the Prarabrahma' the combined manifested entity under the action of five pranaas, namely;

Praan, Apaan, Samaan, Udaan and Vyaan must represent the so called 'Jeeva or Jeevatmaa' the individual incarnate from modified fields of the primary Parabrahma, formed under particular characteristic sequence of combinations of the five bases, which formulate an information template for synthesis of particular proteins, hormones, enzymes and other bio-molecules required by the organism for coming into its characteristic shape, form and function for independent existence. The sequence of bases in a portion of a DNA molecule, called a gene, carries the instructions needed to assemble a protein. In my personal opinion, the secret of the exclusive essential combinations of Adenine with only Thymine and Cytosine with only Guanine bases and the molecular blue-prints they form hide the mechanism for self-generating, assembly and coming into form of the essentially required organs and complementary, functional, physiological systems in any organism under the influence of epigenetic and morphogenetic fields, because biological cells read genetic code more like a script to be interpreted than a blueprint that replicates the same result each time. *(Reference: Nessa Carey)*

The proverbial churning of the oceanic *'Samudra'* has been described to have continued for well over thousand years from its initiation. The proverbial Serpent that has been described in the Puranic story and used as a rope for churning the primordial cosmic ocean was in most possibility, the extremely powerful 'Kristian Birkland Currents' *(See Figures 2-4)* that disrupted the cosmic ocean at billions and billions of volts. These electromagnetic currents move in coiled serpentine forms and therefore the description and mention of a 'Serpent' in the story of *'Samudra Manthan'*, used in the churning of the evolving, unstable, primordial ocean. The Author has earlier described 'Vishnu' as the Universal Cosmic electrostatic potential energy continuum [3]. And 'Vishnu' has always been described and depicted in *Sanatan Vedic* literature to be resting over a coiled- serpentine bed (Kristian Birkland' currents). The above description / explanation of the concept of *Samudra Manthan* therefore fits very well and appears scientifically logical with the modern theories on the structure of matter. In my considered opinion, the "structurally stabilized seeds" of all the fourteen jewels, emerging from the churning of the ocean of electrically charged continuum, actually found their physical shape, coming into form and existence, when perfectly conducive, epigenetic and morphogenetic conditions for their physical manifestation into definite forms were found on a planet like the Earth.

That leaves a likely possibility for the origin of life and living organisms in some remote corner of the space in the universe and existence of the seeds of life, dispersed everywhere in the universe. Perhaps detection of important life generating organic amino acids and water molecules in the tails of comets and soils of Mars and the Earth's moon (now) hold a possibility of the extra-terrestrial or exobiological origin of life on Earth. Personally to me, not all the fourteen jewels, which are described to had emerged from the *'Samudra Manthan'* seem scientifically logical and may have been introduced into the list at some later date without scientific discrimination. It is the existence of the morphogenetic fields on a planet like the Earth, conducive for possibly allowing emergence, growth, manifestation, proliferation, self-generation, self-replication and sustenance of those organic molecules into various forms and kinds of life to possibly happen. I would like to mention here about the work of Joel Sternheimer in France *(Joël Sternheimer– Wikipédia, https:// fr.wikipedia.org › wiki › Joël_..)* on frequencies of vibrations of protein crystals and their combinations into musical notes effecting emergence, growth and early maturity in plants as a possible clue in this direction.

References

1. 'Higgs Force: Cosmic Symmetry Shattered. The story of the greatest scientific discovery for 50 years. By Nicholas Mee, Quantum Wave Publishing, 2012, pp 482. ISBN (PB): 978-0-9572746-1-7.

2. 'At the Edge of Time: Exploring the mysteries of our universe's first seconds'. By Dan Hooper. Princeton University Press, 2019, pp233.

3. 'A Scientific Look at the Concepts of Soul, Rebirth, Work and the Law of Karma: An Attempted Synthesis' By A. V. Moharir, 2019, Zorba Books, Gurugram, India, pp 136.

4. 'The Mighty Electron Recycles All' By James Morgia, 2001, Trafford Publishing, Canada, pp 98.

5. 'The use of the proper time in quantum electrodynamics 1' By Nambu Yoichiro, Progress of Theoretical Physics. 1950, 5 (1): 82–94. Bibcode:1950PThPh...5..82N.doi:10.1143/PTP/5.1.82.

6. 'The Epigenetic Revolution: How Modern Biology is Rewriting Our Understanding of Genetics, Disease and Inheritance' Nessa Carey, Iconbooks, 2012.

The Correlative Scientific Concepts of Lord 'Dattatreya' and the 'Ardha Nari – Nateshwar' from the 'Sanatan Vedic Philosophy': A Note for Discussion

Figure 1. A Statue of Lord Dattatreya. *(Picture credit-Internet free download).*

Lord Dattatreya, symbolizes the combined manifestation of the three traditionally, known forces of nature, that generate, operate (sustain) and destroy (GOD) all material creation in the Universe. Modern physics recognizes four forces in nature namely; weak interaction, strong interaction, gravitation and electromagnetism. The weak and strong interactions are essentially of the same kind except in the range of operation of them. That leaves only three kinds of fundamental forces in nature to contend with. The *'Rishis'* of the Vedic times (25,000 years BC) were perhaps aware of these four fundamental forces of nature which have been recognized by modern science. If the so called imaginary personified *Ishwar / Parmatma* / Creator / GOD as an individual, indeed exists, then he/she has only these four natural forces at his/her disposal to create both the animate and inanimate material universe. In the *Sanatan Vedic* literature, Dattatreya represents combined manifestation of three deities namely; the Brahma, Vishnu and Mahesh. Individually, Vishnu *'Devata'* (Figure 2) who symbolizes the universal cosmic electric potential energy continuum has always been depicted as a personified creator with four arms / hands which represent the four fundamental forces of nature as his only tools for material creation. For that matter, all the *Devata* and their feminine complementary counterpart deities as *Devi*, have also been primarily depicted with four arms. The clear message being that the manifestation and operation of the *Devata* or *Devi* is totally limited by the four forces of nature. These four forces are perpetually in continual operation together in tandem. It is our carelessness that we never looked to our symbolic representations from scientific perspectives and only looked to them as emotionally dogmatic religious symbols of belief. All this prevailed because of continual onslaught and foreign aggressions with deliberate and intentional destruction of our superlative knowledge gathering educational and training schools in areas under control of these aggressors. Even after independence of the country in 1947, intentional continuation of the British education policies, primarily in the hands of anti-*Sanatan*, Muslim ministers, in charge of education portfolio. And they intentionally ignored the correction and reform of our educational and historical distortion done by the Muslim invaders and by the colonial British rulers for centuries.

Figure 2. Vishnu *Devata*, representing the universal cosmic electric energy potential continuum and the creator with only four arms (indicating four fundamental forces of nature as his only tools for creation of the material world). *(Picture credit-Pinterest-Free Download)*.

Figure 3 given below, represents another popular depiction of Vishnu *Devata* in Sanatan philosophy as 'Sheyshashayee-Vishnu' meaning Vishnu sleeping over a huge bed of coiled serpent and his feminine consort Lakshmi sitting at his feet and Brahma emerging from his navel. To me, this picture is not an ordinary representation but clearly displays the most modern scientific understanding of the structure of the universe. The 'coiled serpent' forming the bed of Vishnu represents the modern 'Kristian Birkland Universal Electric Currents' of billions of volts that incessantly flow in coiled trajectories, within and between billions of individual galaxies in the universe and connecting each other. Electric current, representing a flow of negatively charged 'electrons' which are dispersed in the entire universe are the primary constituents of all the visible and invisible matter in the universe. Electrons are responsible for the formation and destruction of all kinds of material (both inanimate and animate) structures formed with elemental building blocks called the atoms in the universe. Such orderly material creation is attributed to be the handiwork of the Lord 'Brahma'. Moreover, 'electrons' are known to be the most stable and indestructible particles in nature with a life span of **1066** years. And this life-span of electrons is more than the estimated life- span of the entire universe. The ocean, on which the giant serpent is floating, factually represents the 'cosmic electric potential continuum' and the entire universe is now known to be electric in nature. With this, it is marvelous and amazing to understand that the *'Rishis'* of the Sanatan Vedic period were certainly aware of the incessant flow of electric currents, known today as the 'Kristian Birkland Currents' within and between galaxies and binding them together, in a continuum of energy and matter **(Figure 4)**. In case of Earth, 'Kristian Birkland Currents' connect the ionosphere with the magnetosphere and channel the energetic solar plasmatic wind energy into the Earth's uppermost atmosphere and to the subsequent layers below.

A magnetosphere of a planet is a region which is heavily influenced by the planet's magnetic field. Earth has relatively the strongest magnetosphere as compared to the other planets of our solar system. The Earth's magnetosphere is a vast cocoon shaped space, which has played a very crucial role evolving and sustaining life and a habitable planet. All life- forms on Earth evolved and developed and continue to do so under the protection of this magnetic environment. The magnetosphere shields our home planet from the incessant blast of very strong solar winds and energetic cosmic particulate radiations, as well as erosion of the atmosphere from the energetic winds– consisting of charged particles streaming off the 'Coronal Mass Ejections' (CME) from the Sun.

Earth's magnetosphere is the part of a dynamic, interconnected system that continually responds sympathetically to solar, planetary, and interstellar conditions. The magnetosphere is generated by the convective motion of the charged, molten iron core lying far below the outer surface of a solid crust. Constant bombardment by the solar wind, compresses the sun-facing side of our magnetic field. The sun-facing side, or dayside, extends a distance of about six to 10 times the radius of the Earth. The side of the magnetosphere facing away from the Sun - the night-side, stretches out into a long extended magnetic-tail, which fluctuates in length to several hundred times the radius of the Earth even beyond orbit of the Moon around Earth. All life-forms on the Earth therefore, are always fighting an incessant battle for their survival against the onslaught of cosmic and solar radiations by continuously adjusting their physiology through *in-vivo* synthesis and release of specific hormones, proteins and other bio- chemicals as individual strategy for survival by maintaining a state of balance or homeostasis, sustained and supported by the epigenetic electrostatic potential gradient surrounding them. Behavioral fluctuations under the influence of such dynamic adjustments for survival observed in the organisms are attributed as their fluctuating 'Mind'.

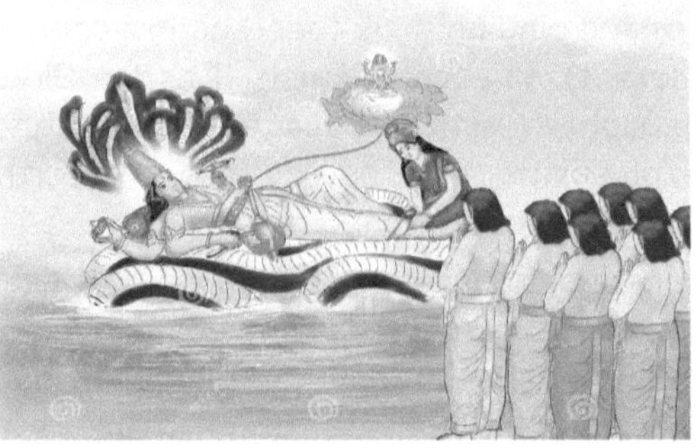

Figure 3. Lord Vishnu *Devata* depicted in Sanatan philosophy as sleeping over a giant serpent floating in the ocean (*Picture Credit- Pinterest-Free Downloads*)

With weak and strong interactions being essentially of similar kind and nature except in the range of their operation between sub-atomic and nuclear particles present within and around the nuclei of atoms, we are left with three forces that are important in nuclear and particle physics. The weak force appears to be very different from the electromagnetic force. It is much weaker and acts over a very short range. Electromagnetic force diminishes with distance in accordance with the inverse square law, such that at twice the distance the force will have only a quarter of its original strength. Although the electromagnetic force falls away steadily in this way, it never falls to zero and therefore has an unlimited range. The weak force on the contrary has a range which is much smaller than the size of an atomic nucleus and operates distinctly different than the electromagnetic force. The electro-weak (GWS) theory propounded in 1960 by Sheldon Glashow, Steven Weinberg and Abdus Salam has however unified the electromagnetism and the weak force and won the 1979 Nobel Prize in Physics [1]. The main feature of the GWS theory is that at extremely high temperatures the electromagnetic and weak forces are two components of a single force, the electroweak force.

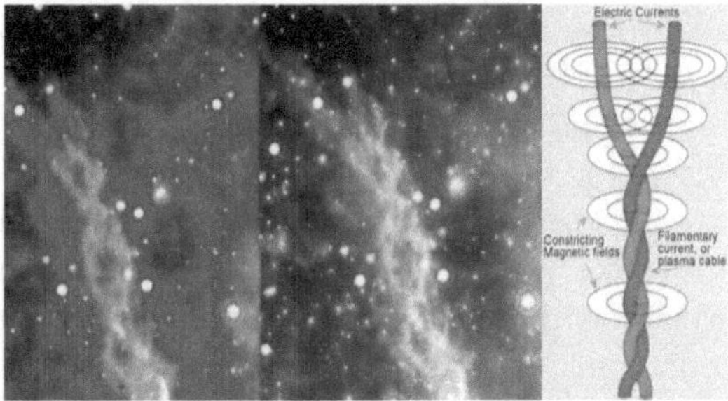

Figure 4. Photographs of the factual helical flow of filamentous 'Kristian Birkland Currents' in the universe. *(image credit-Google search)*

The symmetry between the two forces would only be apparent at trillions of degrees temperatures that could only have occurred when the Big Bang happened and the universe came into existence about 13.7 billion years ago. At lower temperatures the symmetry between the forces is broken; electromagnetism remains a long-range force and weak force as extremely short range one 1. Lord *Dattatreya* (Composit of Brahma, Vishnu and Mahesh) represents the factual reality of apparently three (four) forces which are primarily responsible for re-cyclic creation, sustenance and destruction of all inanimate and animate material in nature. It is incredible that every phenomenon we see in the universe can be explained by just four forces. It would be even more remarkable if the behavior of these four forces can be explained by one single theory based on quantum physics 1 – a dream, for which Albert Einstein spent nearly three quarter of his life in this pursuit. Einstein's dream and intellectual efforts by several others have culminated into evolving the Standard Model of Elementary Particle Physics that has integrated three of the four fundamental natural forces; electromagnetic, weak and strong interactions together. Although, integration of gravitational force still remains distant, the standard model has emerged as the most successful theory so far in classifying all known elementary particles with experimental confirmation of the existence of quarks. Further, the discovery of the top quark (1995), the tau neutrino (2000), and the Higgs boson, the proverbial 'GOD–particle' in 2012 have added more credence to the Standard Model despite several shortfalls e.g. its inability to explain baryon asymmetry, integration of full theory of gravitation and general relativity and accelerating expansion of the universe and existence of dark matter particle. It also does not explain the neutrino oscillations and their non-zero masses.

The operative, super-symmetrical parts of these three primary forces for action in the Indian philosophy have been depicted and symbolized by their three corresponding female deities, namely, Saraswati with Brahma, Lakshmi with Vishnu and Parvati with Mahesh or Shiva. Saraswati, the operative counterpart of Brahma, the creator therefore symbolizes the presiding deity for rhythm, rhythmic periodicity, harmony, peace, tranquility, learning, wisdom and knowledge. This is clearly obvious because it is our common experience that no orderly creative work (construction, structure formation etc) can ever be accomplished without these quality requirements being in place. In short, without, harmony, peace, rhythm, knowledge and wisdom, Brahma cannot create anything. And Brahma is primarily responsible for bringing about every specific material creation from energy and the atoms of only 118 different kinds, so far available in the universe **2**. And all kinds of atoms as the fundamental quantum entities constitute perpetual harmonic oscillators. Vishnu, the sustainer of creation represents the highest universal continuum of cosmic electric potential energy. Vishnu means one who pervades; one who enters into everything that exists. Today we know that the negatively charged particles called 'Electron' are the common constituent of all matter and incidentally that of atoms. So he (Vishnu) is both, the transcendent as well as the immanent reality of the universe. He is the inner cause and power by which everything in the universe exists and we know that it is the electron that brings about combinations of different atoms together in forming various kinds of compounds and structures. Higher the value of the potential energy, higher is the capacity to create and perform work and consequently higher the scope for generating and creating material wealth. Modern physics tells us that no material structure (animate or the inanimate) is possible to exist without electric charge, which pervades the entire cosmos. The whole universe today is known to be electrical in nature **3** and functions of all organic and living organisms are known to be done as result of electric current flowing through millions of ion-channels within body and organ systems of the organisms **4, 5, 6**. That leads me to think that it may indeed be the 'electric charge' that most possibly represents the enigmatic proverbial 'wild goose' called 'Soul', which man has been searching for and holding dear to his/ her heart for thousands of years **7** ? It is our common knowledge that even highest electrostatic potential generated needs orderly regulation and control for its flow through step- up or step- down transformers and grid systems for distribution to various locations to make it produce useful work.

Therefore, Mahalakshmi or Lakshmi, the counterpart female deity of Vishnu (universal cosmic electrostatic potential energy) obviously symbolizes wealth because it is only with higher accumulation of potential energy and its controlled regulation and distribution, there is any possibility to generate the capacity to perform orderly work and create wealth. Otherwise millions and billions of volts of electric potential generated in the earth's atmosphere in the form of lightening is always a disaster. All battles and wars that have been fought throughout the history of human civilizations, irrespective of the declared pretext, purpose or reasons for those fights, have indeed been fought for control of energy resources and nothing else. Lastly, Mahesh or Shiva as a mighty destroyer, possibly symbolizes the Gravitational force in nature which is often destructive. It is the root cause for the accumulation of matter in the universe and for all disturbances as a result of such accumulation on cosmic scale in the universe. The dormant potential state of this mighty force of nature within human body has been identified and symbolized by the 'Kundalini' that lies at the base of the spinal cord. Everything concerned with human spirituality and spiritual life, call it by whatever fanciful synonymous name such as; samadhi, maha-samadhi, nirvana, moksha, communion, union, kaivalya, liberation, bliss or tranquility etc., is related to the awakening of 'Kundalini' within body. Active Manifestation of 'Kundalini' force, depending upon the purpose of its use; in potential capacity generation, continued sustenance or abrupt destruction, are known respectively by the names of – Mahalakshmi, Saraswati and Parvati. No wonder the female operative counterpart of gravitational force should be represented by the most fearful, ruthless, quick, abrupt, thunderously chaotic deity in action, called by the name of Parvati. Other imaginatively perpetuated variations of this force are known by the names of Kali, Maha-Kali, Chandi, Mahishasura Mardini or Durga. In the Tantrik literature, when Kundalini force is awakened but cannot be handled, it is called the Kali. When it can be handled and used for some beneficial purpose and we become powerful on account of it, it is called the Durga. Both, Kali or Durga, because of their unpredictable potential destructive power are the most worshiped, feared and appeased deities for seeking protection to life and property. Both Kali and Durga are indeed the attributes of inner states of human mind / physiology / psychology and behavior 8. The trinity Brahma, Vishnu and Mahesh (Shiv) along with their female counterparts, always simultaneously remain in operation in nature together in tandem and coherence. In case of any weakening of any one of these three forces under any circumstances, the relatively stronger of the remaining two forces, becomes the dominant one and its effect is visualized in action as per its basic nature. In an attempt to seek the scientific truth and meaning contained in the symbolic representation, observation of above correlations between the concept of the Lord Dattatreya from the Sanatan (Indian) Philosophy with modern scientific theory of the physical structure of matter, we only feel dismayed with owe and nothing else.

As scientists uncover more and more of the secrets of the universe expressed in symbolic representations and personified deities, we realize the insignificance of the Earth in the universal scheme of things. And it is the indomitable spirit of inquiry, curiosity and urge of human beings and our brain which not only defines us but even connects us to universe and to each other.

BRAHMA	VISHNU	SHIVA
Most Gyanwaan (He is having Goddess Vidya as his consort.)	Most Dhanwaan (He is having Goddess Lakshmi as his consort.)	Most Balwaan (He is having Goddess Shakti as his consort.)
Lord of science & technology	Lord of commerce & politics	Lord of arts & sports
God of Kindness & Positiveness (Even God Vishnu & God Shiva worship God Brahma for Positiveness.)	God of Righteousness & Success (Even God Brahma & God Shiva worship God Vishnu for Success.)	God of Justice & Fitness (Even God Vishnu & God Brahma worship God Shiva for Fitness.)
He is Jeevan-daata & Deerghaayu-daata (He is Overlord of Maharshi Brahaspati & all other celestial Rishi-Muni)	He is Ann-daata & Sukh-daata (He is Overlord of Indradev, Agnidev, Sooryadev, Vayudev, Varunadev & all nature Gods.)	He is Dhand-daata & Mrityu-daata (He is Overlord of Shanidev, Yamraj, Nagraj and all Bhutas & Pishachas.)
God of Creation	God of Preservation	God of Destruction for Betterment

Figure 5. Characteristic attributes of Brahma, Vishnu and Shiva as described in the Sanatan Vedic Literature (*Picture Credit- Pinterest Free downloads*)

A quantum physical description of the universe

Quantum physics is showing that everything in the universe is 'energy' and 'electrical currents'. Electric currents constitute the movement of negatively charged electrons. Science also says that electrons behave like waves in a sea of energy. According to Stuart Hameroff, Director of the Center for Consciousness, empty space in the universe is not empty. There is something there. If we go down the scale in the emptiness, we come to a 'fundamental level' of space-time geometry, where we find an 'information-pattern'- *the Planck scale* which has been there ever since the Big-Bang occurred. And according to Fred Alan Wolf, "there is no such thing as an empty space. When we go down-down-down-there is vibrations- stuff popping- invisible connections- called entanglement". John Hagelin, another scientist describes it as an invisible state-like a thought wave OR a quantum wave function spread over space and time. Not a wave of matter but a wave in a universal ocean-an ocean of pure potentiality-a unified superstring field, of which we are all made of". The empty space in between stars and planets is not empty but filled with energy in small packets called quarks and leptons surfing on an ocean of pure consciousness. In approaching down from the DNA to the molecules to the atoms to the sub-atomic particles to the smallest particles, we find only energy on top of the 'unified field' an ocean of universal consciousness. And Charles F Haanel in 1912 wrote in his unusual book- 'The Master Key System'- "In the atmosphere we find heat, light and energy. Each realm becomes more and more spiritual as we pass from the visible to the invisible, from the coarse to the fine, from low potentiality to high potentiality. When we reach the invisible we find energy in its purest and most volatile state".

Hassim Haramein, Director of Research at the Hawaii Institute for Unified Physics and profounder of the 'Holofractographic Universe', says that –'everything in the universe is connected through the protons in each atom' Protons (as Hydrogen atoms) are also the most widely distributed particles in the universe. Haramein further goes on to say that –'Within every proton, every subatomic particle in the nucleus of atoms is all the energy, all the informatoin of all other atoms in the universe. So when we go within, we actually connect with that oneness, the connectivity of all things. In short, the entire universe is like a giant feedback loop in itself. ALL MATTER has infinity at its center and the definition of infinite density is a BLACK HOLE. That implies that every cell, every atom, every proton and so on is a mini black hole. These black holes both contract and radiate. All matter has a radiated side and a contracted side. These two sides of the same coin are connected by the event horizon or the rim of the black hole, where there is an exchange of energy taking place between the radiated and the contracted sides. Infinite density at the center of everything that spins; every atom, every particle, every planet, every galaxy provides the necessary torque embedded in the space- time manifold to keep everything perpetually spinning. And when we have massive energy or information 'feedback –loop' with itself, we have the definition of 'consciousness' in the form of a- Conscious Energy Field.

Humans are made of the same kind of stuff that everything else is made of in the universe. The truth of this statement realized today by modern science was actually pronounced by the Sanatan Vedic Philosophy thousands of years before now when it said- *"Pindi Tey Brahmandee"*, what is present in the human body is the same what is present in the universe OR what is present in the universe the same exists within human body. Going down the scale within a human body also, we find cells, molecules, atoms, sub-atomic particles and pure energy. Further, the whole universe if made up of pure energy and at this level everything is in a state of vibrations. Therefore, we are all made of this energy and the packets of this energy are physically surfing in the sea of universal consciousness. From this perspective point of view, it would logically be very clear that – *We all are not only connected with each other but are living in a conscious thought universe*. Under this situation, the intangible world affects the tangible world that we experience and the spiritual world affects the physical world.

In brief, what the modern 'Quantum Physics' tells us can be summarized as follows;

1. Particles are mutually entangled, connected and they are space separated and time separated. And since everything was entangled at the moment the 'Big Bang' occurred, it means everything is still 'touching' each other. And Space is just a construct that gives us an illusion that there are separate objects.

2. Scientists in the field of Quantum Physics have to explore on staggeringly small scales when they move down the dimensions from the cells to molecules to the atoms and then to the sub-atomic levels to the electrons, protons and then to the quarks,

bosons, leptons and so on. What do they observe being that a force appears to be present even at a temperature of absolute zero (-2730 Celcius) at which all forms of energy vanish, which is called the Zero Point Field. That indicates that even below the level of energy, there is still something more basic. The field at this level (at – 2730 Celcius) is not really so called 'energy' nor it is an 'empty space'. Quantum Physicists describe this as a 'field of information' OR the 'ocean', a 'sea of pure consciousness' from which energy appears to arise. In my personal opinion this is perhaps what has been described in the *Sanatan* Philosophy to be the factual *'Hiranyagarbh'*.

3. The matter that we physically perceive is made out of atoms of only 118 different kinds (known so far) and atoms in turn are made of energy that arises out of the **Pure Consciousness** (Zero Point Field) or the **'Hiranyagarbha'** in the language of *Sanatan Vedic* Philosophy.

4. The phrase that we often use – 'that everything is energy' essentially mean that everything has its own vibrational frequency of oscillation.

5. Everything is oscillating because oscillation is the mechanism that creates matter from an oscillating pulse with consciousness at its root.

6. Matter is not structurally continuous nor solid. The appearance is however achieved by points of energy oscillating from positive to negative at varying frequencies e.g. the pixels on a television screen. From the infinite to the finite (manifested), everything is created by a pulse (vibration) which cannot stop.

7. We say everything vibrates or oscillates because vibration relates to the physical world as it is a movement.

8. All is actually MIND, as the first law of the universe states. And in an abstract mind, everything that ever 'moves' is perspective. That is movement by definition and it is not physical. The One Cosmic Mind is conscious and is shifting perspective all the time. That gives rise to the oscillation at varying frequencies which gives matter.

9. Therefore CONSCIOUSNESS is what the universe is made of and Matter and Energy merely represent two forms that consciousness can take.

References

1. 'Higgs Force : Cosmic Symmetry Shattered' The Story of the Greatest Scientific Discovery for 50 Years. Nicholas Mee, Quantum Wave Publishing, 2012.

2. 'Natures Building Blocks' An A-Z Guide to Elements, Oxford University Press, 2002.

3. 'Electric Universe: How Electricity Switched on the Modern World' David Bodanis, ABACUS, 2005.

4. 'The Electric Sky: A Challenge to the Myths of Modern Astronomy' Donald E.Scott, Mikamar Publishing, 2 nd edition, 2012.

5. 'The Body Electric:Electromagnetism and the Foundation of Life', Robert O. Becker and Gary Selden, William Morrow Harper Collins Publishers, 1985.

6. 'Spark of Life: Electricity in the Human Body' Frances Ashcroft, Penguine Books, 2012.

7. 'A Scientific Look at the Concepts of Soul, Rebirth, Work and the Law of Karma: An Attempted Synthesis' Anil Vishnu Moharir, Zorba Books, Gurugram, India, 2019.

8. For more detailed description, the readers are directed to read- 'Kundalini Tantra' by Swami Satyanand Saraswati, Yoga Publication Trust, Munger, Bihar, India, 2002.

9. In writing this article I have drawn heavily with apology for interpretations on the abstracted gist of the television series- Cosmos: A Personal Voyage by Carl Edward Sagan. Who are we? Why are we here? Where are we going? Wheredo we come from in this universe?

10. 'Higgs Force: Cosmic Symmetry Shattered. The Story of the greatest discoveryof fifty years'. Mee, Nicholas, 2012, Quantum Wave Publishing.

11. 'Prana Vidya' From the teachings of Swami Satyanand Saraswati, Swami Niranjanand Saraswati, 2013, Yoga Publications Trust, Munger, Bihar, India

A Correlative Modern Scientific Interpretation of the Concept of 'Prana' as Described in the Book- 'Yog Vidnyan, Part 1, Author-Unknown, Pages 317-322, Published by the Shri Pitambara Peeth, Datia, Madhya Pradesh, 4th Edition, 2014.

"Only a free individual can make a discovery."

Albert Einstein

Introduction

I recently visited the Sri Pitambara Peeth, in Datia, a small town located about 80 km from Gwalior in Madhya Pradesh. While going through the publications and book store of the temple, I happened to pick up three books; 'Yog Vidnyan', Part 1 and Part 2 (4th edition 2011) and 'Swarodaya Vidnyan' (5th edition, 2003), published by the Shri Pitambara Peeth Trust (1). And while reading through the pages of these three books, I was taken aback with the perfectly scientific parallels of description in chaste Hindi with the modern scientific understanding on the structure of matter and energy in relation to the human body and more particularly on the enigmatic universal 'Prana' which is believed to motivate all living organisms. The current article is a result of that exciting stimulus and desire to share my perceptions with the readers. As a professional physicist with life-long experience of working, teaching and conducting research in the field of agriculture and biology, I had recently developed new scientific interpretations on our ancient concepts of soul, rebirth, work and the law of karma, backed up by some deeper correlative insights gained through my research and work experience. The entire creation in the universe is known to be a perpetual interplay of energy and matter and subjects like soul, rebirth and karma had intrigued me and my curiosity since childhood. But I never got to get a clear perception about them even by reading books written by scholars of those times. To me, they all looked similar, perennially repeated, slippery discussions, published under different individual names. They contained no new thoughts, scientifically appealing revelations or interpretations and provided no clear perceptions about the concepts and meaning of soul and rebirth. Much of the description was left to the imagination and the capacity of the readers to interpret. It was here, I had realized then, that a new kind of multi-disciplinary approach was necessary to look at them on the basis of modern scientific theories. Howsoever subtlest, the concept of Prana or the Soul may be, it cannot certainly be something out of the frame of universal creation and its understanding and comprehension. Renowned Astrophysicist Professor Subramaniam Chandrashekhar (NL) has said– "Even the most incomprehensible ideas are indeed comprehensible". I therefore ventured to write a treatise on these complex subjects from a purely multidisciplinary scientific point of view. I am happy that my new scientific interpretations of the ancient concepts are finding positive acceptance by the readers who have bearing in multidisciplinary understanding (*'A Scientific Look at the Concepts of Soul, Rebirth, Work and the Law of Karma: An Attempted Synthesis'*, *Zorba Books, Gurugram, India, pp 136, 2019, ISBN 978-93-88497-84-8*).**(2).**

Some of the most courageous, new premises and conjectures on the concepts of Soul and Rebirth presented in the above mentioned book are as follows;

1. The enigmatic 'Soul' is nothing else but the *de facto primal* electric charge (or electron). All attributes, which have hitherto been assigned to the enigmatic 'Soul' for thousands of years, are equally applicable to the 'electric charge'.
2. 'Souls' of all living organisms remain in continual connection from the moment of their conception, birth to death with the 'Universal electric charge potential continuum' by means of the 'electric energy' mediated through millions of 'ion channels' within and between individual cells, membranes, organs and bodies of living organisms.
3. Rebirth / Reincarnation of individual persons, after their death is technically or scientifically impossible and continues to be a 'Popular Myth' and not a factual truth. However, from the multidisciplinary modern scientific point of view, the concept

of 'Rebirth' merely represents the birth of a new individual, who resembles in his / her characteristics traits with those of someone who had lived in the historical past. And such regeneration / replication of characteristic traits factually arise from the routine self-replication of the DNA and RNA molecules in associated interaction with their epigenetic environments. DNA and RNA are the fundamental basic genetic molecules from which all life forms evolve. Therefore, Rebirth essentially represents an exact or near-exact, cyclic regeneration of characteristic traits through a routine self-replication of the DNA and RNA molecules and it is certainly not the rebirth of any individual after his / her death from the historical past. *The factual meaning of 'Rebirth' therefore is a repeated regeneration of specific characteristic traits in a new born individual and certainly not the 'physical return to rebirth' of anyone who had died in the past.* **In short, it is the rebirth of specific human traits 'Guna-r-janma' and not the rebirth of a dead individual 'Poona-r-janma'.** Even otherwise, in considering cases of possible rebirth of any historical person, we only compare and contrast the characteristic traits and qualities and certainly not the physical appearances. And in the absence of a historical record or a documented, evidence for comparison, the concept of rebirth indeed loses all its meaning.

4. The origin and operation of the 'Universal Law of Karma' has been explained on the basis of molecular genetics. A recently discovered, fundamental, dynamic process of DNA-methylation, perpetually going on in every individual cell of all living organisms, as its 'strategic-mechanism for survival' under changing environmental conditions, has been functionally correlated with the working of the 'personified mythological character of 'Chitragupta'. It is believed that 'Chitragupta', secretly writes a detailed record of all the work done *(interactions with environment)* by the living organism all through its life from birth to death. This description of the working of 'Chitragupta' is akin, analogous and parallel to the continuous, dynamic and hidden process of DNA-methylation that goes on within all the living biological cells. DNA-methylation process is a continual mechanism that keeps on adjusting the survival strategy for

the cell against continuously changing *epi-genetic* environment outside the body of the organism.

A prelude to the discussion

Cosmologists and Astrophysicists declare that the entire universe is filled with protons and electrons and the universe is essentially electrical in nature **(3)**. Moreover, the inter-galactic space and that within individual galaxies is not only inter connected but is filled with electrically charged ionized gaseous plasma through which the 'Birkland electric currents', circulate. All material in the universe is made up of the elementary units of material called the atoms, which are available in only 118 different kinds as have been listed in the Periodic Table of elements. Atoms of different elements combine with one another by either sharing or transferring negative electrons between individual atoms to build various compounds with characteristic properties. Electrons again are responsible for not only sustaining a certain structural compound built under specific environmental and epigenetic conditions but also for its disintegration into the constituent atoms. This is true not only in case of the inanimate matter but also in case of what is described as the animate/ living / conscious biological material. Electrons are known to be the common constituent of all atoms and also the most stable particle in the universe without any decay. Life of electron has been estimated to be 10^{66} years and this time span is longer than the life of universe itself. Electrons are universally dispersed and the amount of electric charge on them is a universally constant and quantized. When released from any animate or inanimate object or organism, they simply merge into the atmosphere and become part of the universal (Consciousness) continuum / expanse. Like the negatively charged electrons, a positively charged hydrogen proton, has the same physical and chemical characteristic anywhere in the universe. Now, if we pause, ponder, carefully compare, contrast and correlate, we would see that the characteristic attributes and properties of electrons are identical to what have traditionally been described in relation to the enigmatic 'Soul' since centuries in the historical past. Developments in modern physics and the 'Standard Model of Particle Physics' do not contradict this interpretation. This is the reason, why the author *(A V Moharir)* very courageously propounds in his book*, that what is described as the 'Soul' and the prime mover of all the living conscious organisms is nothing else but the *de facto* electric charge (electron). We have only lost courage to recognize this fact under the weight of the dogmatic belief and blind faith in the illusion of knowledge described by the religious or philosopher stalwarts since time immemorial at the back of our sub-conscious mind. James Morgia **(4)** emphatically declares that it is the "Mighty Electron' that recycles everything in the universe as an integral part of the recycle process in nature.

A correlative comparison

With the above prelude in our mind, let us now see, what the authoritative 'Ved-Vidnyan' Book from the Pitambara Peeth explain about 'Prana or Soul' the driving force of all the living creatures on Earth? The important five pages from this book, describing Prana, have been reproduced below for the convenience of the readers. The significant lines from these five pages have been highlighted to draw the attention of the readers to understand, compare, identify and critically analyze, the information conveyed in these highlighted lines, in correlation with modern scientific terminologies. The most essential scientific information revealed from the lines described in this book has been logically correlated and summarized below;

1. Breathing in and breathing out is connected to the *'Para-bramha'* the universal soul. (*That is, all living beings are connected to the universal soul/ consciousness*).

2. Oxygen breathed inside, is the carrier of the universal soul. *Here as we know, that oxygen is merely a carrier of electrons which are exchanged to the red blood cells which are pumped and circulated throughout the body by means of the heart through blood arteries, veins and vesicles. Electrons, exchanged with the outer membranes of cells, generate electric potential difference and trigger all the metabolic bio-chemical activities within the cells.*

   It is known that all living organisms have; (a) respiratory (b) digestive (c) metabolic (d) excretory (e) mental and psychic and (f) procreative systems to function for independent existence. It is the *Prana* that goes within the body and operates all these systems. *Prana* enters inside the body through the nostrils and mouth, every moment from the first breath at birth to the last breath on death and goes out. It is the nectar of life. As long as *Prana* enters, resides and circulates within the body, the body does not decay, perish and die. Academically, *Prana* circulates within body as '*Vital Vayu*' (nerve force) but its aboriginal form is a kind of the Sun. The term '*Vayu*' is often extended to include any kind of electromotive or molecular force. *Vayu* is a self-originated principle in the human and all animated conscious organisms. *Vayu* in Sanskrit has also been described popularly as, 'A Vile', mischievous, troublesome, and hateful and a pestilent child. Considering the fact that the earth being a part and parcel of the solar system and of our galaxy at large, the atmosphere on the earth is dynamically changing every moment depending upon the flux of energy it receives both from the Sun, the Moon and our entire galaxy. As a result, the bodies of all living organisms irrespective of species remain engaged in perpetually adjusting their internal metabolism against the changing Solar electron flux and corresponding epigenetic environmental conditions more as a part of their survival strategies to remain in constant connection with the universal *Prana / Soul*. Dynamic adjustments made against changing environment for survival through DNA-methylation process is indeed the record of the work done by all individual cells in their lives. And this is the hidden record keeping process, the personified mythological character described as the '*Chitragupta*'.

Prana determines the origin, growth, sustenance and disintegration of all animated organisms (that include all life forms from air, land and aquatic origin). Although *Prana* itself is invisible, its work is patent and manifest. It is cold, light, mobile, dry, piercing and all-pervading in the universe. It is instantaneous in its action and radiates or courses through the body of organisms in **constant currents**. The *Prana*, manifests itself within the body in ten different kinds / forms/ states/ nature and behavior, depending on the function, they perform in the body system. These are named as; *Prana, Vyan, Udan, Saman, Apaan, Nag, Kurma, Krukal, Devadatta and Dhannanjaya*. Although all these ten kinds of *Prana* are essentially the same, the relatively most important five are; the *Prana, Udan, Vyan, Samaan and Apaan*. Their specific locations within human body and area of operation have long been precisely described by Deerghatama Rishi in detail.

3. Sequentially describing, *Prana* stays operational in the head and all organs and specific body actions, such as spitting, sneezing, burping, exhalation, food intake from the mouth are ascribed to it *(Prana).*

4. *Udaan Prana* is primarily located and remains operational within chest, throat, nostrils, neck and navel. Inclination, attitude. Memory, force, performance, speech, prayer, attempt are some of the main functions of human behavior ascribed to it.

5. *Vyan Prana* is located within the heart and its movement is very quick and speedy. Its domain is above and below the heart and proliferate the entire body.

6. *Saman Prana* concentrates predominantly in and around the stomach, the digestive system and the anus. Intake of food, its digestion, assimilation are the principal functions of Saman Prana.

7. *Apan Prana* is located at the anus and operates from the throat, belly below the navel, the hypogastrium and pubes, a clyster pipe, a tube of bladder or gut with a nozzle. Its main function being excreting semen, menstrual fluid, faces, urine and the baby during child birth.

It would be very clear from the description above that the functions of all the five kinds of *Prana* are akin and parallel to the working of the electrical energy. Just as electrical energy is the prime mover behind operation and working of all the electrical gadgets, irrespective of their function and use, so also the various *Prana,* although called by different names, are fundamentally the same and is the *de facto* electric charge. The *Prana* is also called by different people by different names as the I or Me / Self / Psyche / Astral Body / Conscience / Subtle Body / Spirit / Spiriton/ Subconscious / Super Conscious / Voice of the Heart / *Atma* / *Paramatma* / *Jeeva* / *Jeevatmaa* / Energy-Informational Matrix / Reactive Mind / *Bramha* / *Parabramha* / Consciousness / *Prana* and most recently as the Quantum Monod etc. in essentially describing the same thing popularly known since antiquity as the "SOUL". It is worth standing away from the madding crowd and orthodox views, pause for a while and introspect, if our efforts to realize the enigmatic 'Soul' as we perceive and attempt to realize it, as has been described by celebrated people for thousands of years in the past, may not be a 'proverbial chase for the non-existent wild goose'.

I wish the readers of this write-up, not only see the reason, logic and substance in the given interpretation but also support it from modern scientific point of view.

योग-विज्ञान

(प्रथम भाग)

लेखक

अज्ञात

श्री पीताम्बरा पीठ

दतिया, (मध्य प्रदेश)

(३१६)

ढूंढकर सूर्यलोक को प्राप्त होते हैं वे पुनः जन्म धारण नहीं करते। कारण कि सूर्य ही प्राणों का आश्रय है, वही मोक्ष है, वही अभय पद है। इसलिए कर्म करने वालों को यह परमाश्रय मिला हुआ है। सारांश यह कि प्राण ही सूर्य का रूप है। सूर्य जब अपने आप को खींच लेता है तब प्राणी रूप आदि विभिन्न गुणों से हीन होकर मुक्त हो जाता है क्योंकि प्राणों के द्वारा ही शरीर का सम्बन्ध है। अतएव प्राणों का आश्रय सूर्य इनको खींचकर प्राणी को मुक्त कर देता है।

प्राण की महिमा का वर्णन करते हुए हमारे महान् पुरुषों ने लिखा है कि 'प्राण अग्निरूप से तपता है, सूर्य, मेघ, इन्द, वायु, पृथ्वी, रवि (चन्द्रमा का भोग) यही है, सत् एवं असत् भी यही है एवं यही अमृत है।

यह प्राण ही विराट् रूप होकर गर्भ में रहता है, उत्पन्न होता है एवं अन्य प्राणों से स्थित रहता है। देवों आदि को बल प्राण ही पहुँचाता है, प्राण ही इंद्र है, तेजस्वी होने के कारण प्राण ही रुद्र है, यही रक्षक है, यही सूर्य का रूप धारण किए हुए आकाश में विचरता है, नक्षत्रों का पति है व मेघ रूप होकर वर्षा करता है तथा प्रजा के प्राणों की रक्षा करता है।

इसी प्राण के नियंत्रण का नाम प्राणायाम है। प्राणायाम करते समय सप्त व्याहृति (१) भू (२) भुव (३) स्वः (४) महः (५) जनः (६) तपः (७) सत्यम् सहित गायत्री मंत्र का मन से चिन्तन करता हुआ नेत्रों को बन्द करके पूरक करें व पश्चात् उपर्युक्त मंत्र की तीन आवृत्ति करता हुआ कुम्भक करे, इसके बाद एक बार स्मरण करता हुआ रेचक करे। लेकिन कुछ योगाचार्यों का कहना है कि उक्त मंत्र का ध्यान असम्भव है। अतएव प्रणव का जाप करने से

(३१७)

ही प्राणायाम सिद्ध हो जाता है। प्रणव की संख्या निश्चित करके उससे पूरक करे, उससे चार गुना प्रणव का जप करते हुए कुम्भक करे और पूरक की दुगनी संख्या में रेचक करे। इस अभ्यास से यम, नियम, आसन, धारणा और ध्यान स्वतः सिद्ध हो जाते हैं। इसके उपरांत समाधि प्राप्त हो जाती है व समाधि के द्वारा ईश्वर का साक्षात्कार हो जाता है।

प्राण पूजा स्वात्म पूजा है अतः परमात्मा की एवं चेतन की पूजा है। इस पूजा में जरा भी मन लगाने वाला संसार से पार हो सकता है क्योंकि प्राणवायु ही पंचमहावायुओं में मुख्य होने के कारण मुक्ति को प्रदान करने वाली है। अतएव जो पुरुष प्रणव मंत्र ॐ का जप करते हुए प्राणायाम करता है वह सूर्य में निवास करता है और पापों से मुक्त होकर ब्रह्मलोक में वास करता हुआ परमात्मा में लीन हो जाता है।

प्राण क्या है?

श्रीमद्भगवत् गीता महात्म्य में भी लिखा है कि प्राणायाम परायण पुरुष के इस जन्म के ही क्या पूर्व जन्म तक के पाप नहीं रहते, यही कारण है कि सभी लोग इसे जानने को उत्सुक रहते हैं। अतएव पहले यह जान लेना भी अत्यन्त आवश्यक है कि प्राण क्या है? अस्तु यदि प्राण शब्द की व्याख्या कर दी जाय तो प्राणायाम के अर्थ शीघ्र ही समझ में आ जावेंगे।

उपनिषद् की कथा है कि एक बार शरीर के सभी अभिमानी देवताओं ने अपने—अपने वश की हुई इन्द्रियों द्वारा विचार कराया कि उन सब में कौन श्रेष्ठ है? आकाश, वायु, अग्नि, पृथ्वी, वाणी, मन, चक्षु व श्रोत्र ने अपनी—अपनी महिमा वर्णन करते हुए कहा कि

(३१८)

हम ही इस शरीर को धारण किये हैं। तब प्राण ने कहा अरे मूर्खों! आत्मा के लिये पाँच रूप में विभक्त होकर मैं ही इस शरीर को धारण किये हूँ, परन्तु उनके विश्वास न करने पर जब प्राण शरीर छोड़कर जाने लगा तब सब इन्द्रियाँ नष्ट होने लगी। अतएव जब सभी ने प्राणों को विनय करके रोका तब सब स्थित रह सके। प्रश्नोपनिषद् ने प्राण को 'व्रात्य' कहा है। व्रात्य का अर्थ है जिसके परे कोई न हो। प्राणों के सम्बन्ध में उसमें आगे यह भी कहा है—

'प्राणस्येदं वशे सर्वं त्रिदिवेयत्प्रतिष्ठितं मातेव पुत्रान् रक्षस्व श्रीश्च प्रज्ञां च विधेहि न इति' अर्थात् यह सब प्राण के वश में है और स्वर्ग में जो कुछ है वह है प्राण! तेरे वश में है। हे प्राण! माता के समान पुत्रों का पालन कर। लक्ष्मी एवं सरस्वती व श्री एवं प्रज्ञा को हम दे। इसी प्राण के नियंत्रण को प्राणायाम कहते हैं।

जैसे सम्राट अपने अधीन राजाओं का शासन बाँट देता है इसी प्रकार यह प्राण दूसरे प्राणों को अलग-अलग उपदेश देता है। उपनिषद् में अपान आदि वायु भी प्राण के नाम से पुकारे जाते हैं। उसमें लिखा है कि मुँह व नाक में प्राण वायु रहता है। इस प्राण को सप्ताचीष कहा है क्योंकि दो कान, दो नेत्र, दो नासारंध्र व एक मुँह। यह प्राण की सात अग्नि स्वरूप ज्योतियाँ हैं।

श्रुति का यह महत्वपूर्ण वाक्य है कि जिसने प्राण तत्त्व को जान लिया उसने वेद को जान लिया। इसी कारण वेदान्त सूत्रों में भी यह लिखा है कि श्वास प्रश्वास ही परब्रह्म है। क्योंकि उसी की सहायता से हम सब काम करते हैं। इस ब्रह्मांड में जो कुछ भी शक्ति है प्राण उसका मूल तत्त्व है। प्रकृति की सारी शक्तियों का आधार प्राण ही है अर्थात् मनुष्य व अन्य सब प्रकार की गुप्त व प्रकट शक्तियों का आधार प्राण ही है। प्राण का सम्बन्ध परमात्मा से है। यदि मन के द्वारा कार्य करने वाली प्राण की साधारण

(३१९)

क्रियाओं को अपने वश में कर लें तो हम प्राण के भेद को भली भाँति सीख लेंगे। जो योगी इस भेद को अच्छी तरह जान जाता है वह किसी भी शक्ति से नहीं डरता क्योंकि उसे विश्व की प्रत्येक शक्ति पर पूर्ण अधिकार हो जाता है। प्रलय के समय यह प्राण सूक्ष्म रूप में पड़ा रहता है और प्रलय के पश्चात आकाश में कार्य करना आरम्भ कर देता है जिसके फलस्वरूप तमाम वस्तुओं का निर्माण होता है। प्राण और पदार्थ के मिश्रण से ही ब्रह्मांड और पिंड बनते हैं।

इच्छा शक्ति के अधिकार में विचारों को करके उनके अनुसार श्वास लेने से एक अपूर्व शक्ति प्राप्त हो सकती है। इस शक्ति द्वारा आत्मोन्नति, अपने तथा दूसरों के असाध्य रोग और दुःख दूर किये जा सकते हैं। अपने जीवन में इसका बड़ी सुगमता से प्रयोग किया जा सकता है। कितने ही महात्माओं ने व योगियों ने इसका प्रयोग किया है व कर रहे हैं। प्राणायाम व श्वास सम्बन्धी अन्य क्रियाओं को करके आप भी वैसा कर सकते हैं। प्राणायाम के करते समय प्राण की अदृश्य शक्तियों का अपने अन्दर अनुभव कीजिए। योगी बनकर अपने चारों ओर प्रसन्नता, प्रकाश व शक्ति का अनुभव कीजिए।

प्राण का महत्त्व

महर्षि पिप्पलाद ने भरद्वाज ऋषि से कहा था कि यह प्राणादि जिससे उत्पन्न हुए हैं वह आत्मा इसी शरीर में अंगुष्ठ मात्र होकर हृत्कमल में निवास करता है। सृष्टि के विषय में उसने विचार किया कि सबका आश्रय तो मैं हूँ मेरा आश्रय क्या होगा, तब उसने प्राण की उत्पत्ति की। प्राण से श्रद्धा उत्पन्न की, आकाश, वायु, तेज, जल, पृथ्वी, दशों इन्द्रियों, मन, अन्न, वीर्य, तप, मंत्र, कर्म एवं लोक प्रसिद्ध नामादि रचे। जो इस महाप्राण व इसके महत्त्व को

(३२०)

जानता है वह अमर हो जाता है।

स सप्रीची: स विषूचीर्वसान आवरीवर्ति भुवनेष्वन्तः:

ऋ०वे० ९/१६४/३९/१०/१०६/३

इस मंत्र के द्रष्टा दीर्घतमा ऋषि कह रहे हैं कि मैंने प्राण को देखा है, साक्षात्कार किया है। यह प्राण सब इन्द्रियों का गोपा (रक्षक) है। यह कभी नष्ट होने वाला नहीं है। यह भिन्न-भिन्न मार्गों अर्थात् नाड़ियों के द्वारा आता और जाता है। मुख तथा नासिका के द्वारा क्षण-क्षण यह शरीर में आता है और फिर बाहर चला जाता है। यह प्राण शरीर में अध्यात्म रूप में, वायु के रूप में है, परन्तु अधिदैवत रूप में सूर्य हैं।

इस समस्त विश्व के देव, मनुष्य तथा पशु आदि समग्र प्राणी प्राण वायु के द्वारा व्याप्त हैं। प्राण अमृतरूप है। जब तक इसका देह में वास है, यह शरीर मृत्यु को प्राप्त नहीं होता।

यह प्राण शरीर में स्वधा-अन्न के द्वारा ही स्थित है। यह मलमूत्रादि के निकालने के लिए अधोभाग में जाया करता है। तथा साँस के लिए मुखादि ऊर्ध्व भाग में संचरण किया करता है। अर्थात् वह अपान तथा प्राण के रूप में शरीर में सर्वदा संचार किया करता है। प्राण अमर्त्य है—अर्थात् मृत्यु रहित है, परन्तु वह मरण धर्म वाले शरीर के साथ सदा एक स्थान पर निवास करता है। यह प्राण और शरीर विविध व्यापार सम्पन्न है तथा आपस में विरुद्ध हैं। क्योंकि मृत्यु हो जाने पर शरीर पृथ्वी पर गिर जाता है, परन्तु प्राण ऊपर लोकान्तर में चला जाता है। इन दोनों में देह को मनुष्य अन्न पान के द्वारा बढ़ा सकता है, परन्तु प्राण को अन्न और पान से कोई भी नहीं बढ़ा सकता।

(३२१)

प्राण का स्थान

अन्तःकरण ही प्राण का स्थान है। यद्यपि अन्तःकरण भी एक ही है फिर भी उसके भिन्न-भिन्न कार्यों के अनुसार चार रूप माने जाते हैं। (१) मानस (२) बुद्धि (३) चित्त (४) अहंकार।

वायु दस प्रकार की होती है। (१) प्राण (२) अपान, (३) व्यान (४) उदान (५) समान (६) नाग (७) कूर्म (८) कृकल (९) देवदत्त (१०) धनंजय।

प्राण वायु का आधार अपान वायु है, अपान, व्यान के अधीन है, व्यान, उदान पर अवलम्बित है और उदान का नैसर्गिक सम्बन्ध समान वायु से है। समान वायु की समानता, एकरसता, अखंड रूप से बनी रहे बस इसी में आनन्द, कल्याण और शांति है। उसके असमान होने पर ही काल प्राणी पर अपना अधिकार जमा लेता है।

यद्यपि प्राण एक ही है फिर भी इसके भिन्न-भिन्न कार्यों के अनुसार आगे लिखे पाँच रूप माने जाते हैं।

(१) प्राण (२) उदान (३) व्यान (४) समान और (५) अपान। इसे वृत्त भेद व प्रधान प्राण को मुख्य प्राण कहते हैं। प्राण के रहने का स्थान अन्तःकरण है। उपर्युक्त वायुओं के भिन्न-भिन्न स्थान व कार्य आगे लिखे जाते हैं।

(१) प्राण वायु का स्थान शिर है। हृदय के ऊपर के कार्य प्राण वायु द्वारा होते हैं। थूकना, छींकना, डकार, श्वास को छोड़ना, अन्न प्रवेश आदि इसके कार्य हैं। याद रहे कि श्वास-प्रश्वास प्राण वायु नहीं बल्कि वह प्राण है।

(२) उदान वायु का प्रधान स्थान वक्ष, विचरण स्थान कंठ, नाभि, नासिका व गला है। प्रवृत्ति, स्मृति, बल, पराक्रम, सुमति, वरण,

(३२२)

वाणी व प्रयत्न आदि इसके कार्य हैं।

(३) व्यान का प्रधान स्थान हृदय है। इसका सब अङ्ग में संचार रहता है। बड़ा वेग वाला, नीचे ऊपर को फेंकना, गति, निमेष व उन्मेष आदि इसके कार्य हैं।

(४) समान का स्थान अन्याशय के समीप है। कोष्ठ अर्थात् आमाशय से गुदा तक विचरण करता है। अन्न को ग्रहण, पाचन व अलहदा करता व फेंकना इसका कार्य है।

(५) अपान वायु का स्थान गुदा है। कंठ, वस्ति, मूत्रेन्द्रिय, जानु व योनि में विचरण करता है। वीर्य, मासिक धर्म, मल, मूत्र व गर्भ बाहर निकालना इसके कार्य हैं।

श्वास की गति

मनुष्य के शरीर में आने–जाने वाली श्वास की गति का प्रमाण व उसके निरोध से होने वाले लाभ अलहदा प्रकरण में दिए गए हैं।

प्राणायाम की व्याख्या

पातंजल योग का सूत्र है– 'श्वासप्रश्वासयोर्गतिविच्छेदः प्राणायामः।' यह श्वासायाम योग है प्राणायाम नहीं। श्वास की अपेक्षा प्राणशक्ति अधिक सूक्ष्म है इसलिए सूत्र का अभिप्राय यह मालूम होता है कि श्वासायाम साधने से पीछे प्राणायाम स्वतः होने लगेगा। पातञ्जल योग सूत्र के अध्याय २ सूत्र ४८ की व्याख्या के अनुसार इच्छानुसार श्वाँस लेने और छोड़ने की क्रिया पर अधिकार प्राप्त करने का नाम प्राणायाम है, जो कि आसन सिद्ध होने पर ही प्राप्त होती है।

(३२३)

प्राणायाम एक पूर्ण वैज्ञानिक विद्या है। नासिका द्वारा अन्दर ली जाने वाली साँस को 'श्वास' और नसिका ही से बाहर जाने वाली श्वास को 'प्रश्वास' कहते हैं। श्वास जीवनदाता प्राण का बाह्य तथा स्थूल रूप है। स्थूल श्वास के सूक्ष्म रूप को ही प्राण कहते हैं। स्थूल श्वास के ऊपर नियंत्रण करने से सूक्ष्म प्राण के ऊपर भी नियंत्रण किया जा सकता है। प्राण के ऊपर नियंत्रण होने से मन पर नियंत्रण हो जाता है। प्राण की सहायता बिना मन काम ही नहीं कर सकता। प्राण की गति से ही मन में चंचलता उत्पन्न होती है। यह सूक्ष्म प्राण ही है जिसका मन से घनिष्ठ सम्बन्ध है। श्वास शरीर के लिए उतना ही महत्त्वपूर्ण है जितना कि इंजन का वह पहिया जिसके चलाने से वह चलता और रुक जाता है। जिस तरह ड्राइवर द्वारा उस पहिये के रोकने ही से इंजन के सब कल पुर्जों का काम करना रुक जाता है उसी तरह योगी के श्वास रोकते ही शरीर के सब अंग्र काम करना बन्द कर देते हैं। इसी प्रकार यदि आप स्थूल श्वास पर अधिकार कर सकते हैं तो जीवन दाता प्राण पर भी सफलता पूर्वक पूर्ण अधिकार हो जाएगा। जिस उपास से श्वास और प्रश्वास की गति पर नियंत्रण किया जाता है अर्थात प्राणों के आयाम को प्राणायाम कहते हैं।

गीता अध्याय ४ श्लोक २६ में लिखा है कि अपान वायु में प्राण वायु का तथा प्राण वायु में अपान वायु का प्रवेश करे और फिर प्राण व अपान दोनों की गति को रोके। इसी क्रिया का नाम प्राणायाम है।

योगिराज काकभुशुण्डि जी ने वशिष्ठ जी को बतलाया था कि ९६ मात्रा काल बाहर जाने की तरह यदि प्राण ९६ मात्रा ही भीतर भी लिया जाय तो वह प्राण शरीर के लिए बहुत लाभदायक हो, परन्तु स्वाभादिक रीति से ९२ मात्रा ही प्राण श्वास के साथ अन्दर

References

1. 'Yog Vidnyan' Author Unknown, Part-1, Published by Shri Pitambara Peeth, Datia, Madhya Pradesh, pp 317-322, 4 th Edition, 2014.

2. 'A Scientific Look at the Concept of Soul, Rebirth, Work and the Law of Karma : An Attempted Synthesis' Anil Vishnu Moharir, Zorba Books, Gurugram, Haryana, India, 2019. ISBN 978-93-88497-84-8.

3. 'The Electric Sky: A Challenge to the Myths of Modern Astronomy' Donald E Scott, Mikamar Publishing, Portland, Oregon. 2012, ISBN 978-0-9830966-6-5.

4. 'The Mighty Electron Recycles All' James V. Morgia, 2001, Trafford Publishing. ISBN 1-55212-717-6

Our Connection to the Cosmic Electric Potential Continuum or 'Universal Consciousness' for Existence and Survival: An Attempted Scientific Synthesis

Abstract

In this article an attempt has been made by the author to discuss the processes involved in coming into form as a living human beings in particular and all other life forms in general on earth, without any bias and dogmatic religious beliefs. He has based his discussion purely on modern scientific understanding on matter-energy relationship and their interplay within the scheme of universal creation. In doing so, he has attempted to describe the sequential processes involved in the making of a human child within the womb of its mother in relation to our knowledge, understanding, experience about the existence of the energy power grids within human body, popularly known as the 'Chakras' *(from the 'Sanatan Vedic' Scientific knowledge)* and concluded that as a part and parcel of universal creation, how all the living beings are continually connected to the universal cosmic electric energy continuum. During this discussion, the author has made use of some selective, representative diagrammatic pictures and photographs (downloaded from the free download site of 'Pinterest') to help readers in forming a clear mental perception for their understanding the processes involved at the subtlest levels. Because the subject is extremely complex, relatively subjective for comprehension, depending upon the educational background, training, preparedness and therefore becomes at times controversial. Still, however, the author believes that his readers would find it not only interesting but deeply penetrating to connect our ancient and modern knowledge on the subject in a clear perspective.

Introduction

Every human being and other living organisms, from unicellular bacteria and archaea, to the multi-cellular, multi-organ animals, existing on earth, irrespective of their terrestrial or aquatic origin, constitute a part and parcel of the universal re-cycling of the energy-matter continuum or 'Universal Consciousness'. The frequently observed electromagnetic induction coupling of the solar and terrestrial core is an expression of the universal phenomenon of coupling between celestial cosmic bodies and all kinds of the biological systems existing and surviving on the Earth. Ancient 'Sanatan Vedic Wisdom' from India, which is more than twenty thousand years old, had clearly declared that, "it is not we, who dwell in a universe of gigantic proportions, but the whole universe dwells within us". In short, what is present in the universe is also present within a living human body and *vice versa*, **Figures-1 and 2**.

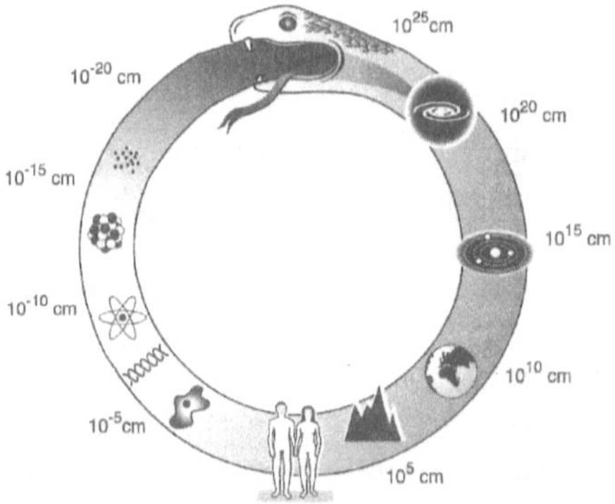

Figure 1. The 'Oraborus'. A graphical illustration indicating the links between the micro-world of particles, nuclei and atoms on (left) and the cosmic macro world on (right) and a perpetually recycling nature of the universe. Reproduced with the permission of the author Professor Martin Rees, from his book- 'Just Six Numbers', Phoenix (1999)

Figure 2. Plasma Gas glows white, lit by a stellar nursery, in this view of a region within the Large Magellanic Cloud, the Milky Way's largest satellite galaxy. Most cosmic gas is not so visible and lies outside of galaxies — in halos surrounding galaxies and in the vast spaces in between. Yet the gas determines galactic life cycles *(Credit NASA)*.

Four forces, namely; weak nuclear interaction, strong nuclear interaction, electromagnetic and gravitation have been recognized to be controlling the entire universal creation, its sustenance and finally its destruction. Physicists, Astrophysicists and Cosmologists assure us, that the entire universe is electrical in nature and the 'universal energy continuum' is nothing but the electrical charge potential continuum of ionized plasma-material that fills the universe and the inter-galactic space. The planet Earth is electrically neutral overall because it contains an equal amount of positive and negative charges. This neutrality arises from a balance between the positive and negative charges carried by protons and electrons respectively of every single atom distributed throughout its various components like the crust, mantle, and core that constitute the Earth. The net charge of the Earth as a whole is essentially zero. Still however, there are localized variations in electric charge distribution on Earth due to factors like thunderstorms, lightning, and the movement of charged particles in the atmosphere. Likewise, according to the Electric Universe theory, the whole universe itself is electrical in nature and challenges the gravity-centric model by asserting that electricity is the primary force shaping the cosmos, instead of gravity. It proposes that an interconnected network of plasma connects every galaxy and that electricity, not gravity, drives all universal celestial interactions **(Figures 2, 3)**.

Figure 3. Hubbell Space Telescope Image of the Clusters of innumerable stars within the Phantom Galaxy with inter connected threads of Birkland (Plasma) currents

According to Dr. Matt Taylor, Astrophysicist at the European Space Agency, "Plasma physics permeates everything". Further, all existing life forms on the Earth, constitute as large masses of self-organized, self-regulated, self-automated, biological, cellular-machines, fully submerged, into the all-pervading, vast universal ocean of electrical potential continuum, **Figure 2 and 3**.

Development and structure of human body

Modern genetics reveals that every human is created when two separate cells (the smallest cell in the human body–the Sperm from male and the biggest cell in the human body- the Egg from female) fuse together to form a 'zygote', in which, cells begin to multiply in an incredibly humble way, starting from a little sac of proteins. **Figure 4 and 5.**

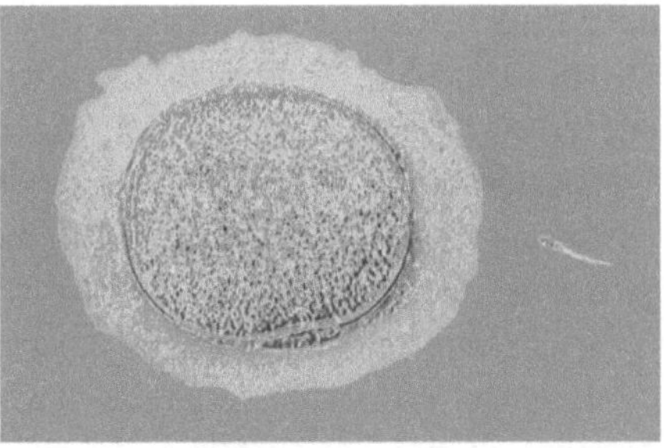

Figure 4. An Optical Microscope image of a Tiny Sperm cell from the Male (On right with a tail) if swimming towards a large Egg cell from the female *(on the Right, Reproduced with apology from the internet web)*

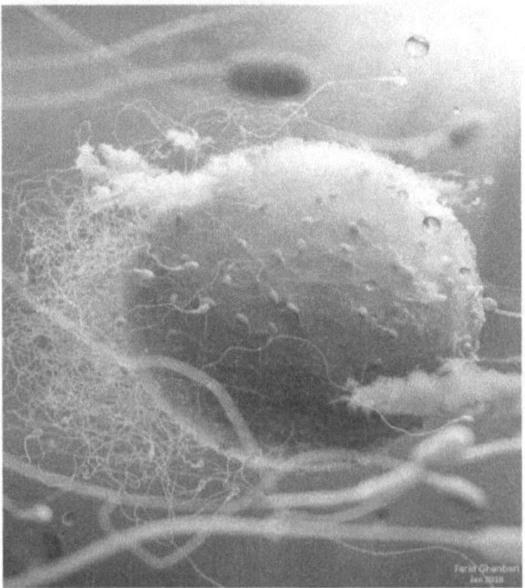

Figure 5. Scanning Electron Microscope picture of a female egg cell surrounded by male sperm cells. Mark their comparative size variation

Within, nearly forty weeks in the uterus, those two original cells of zygote, undergo a miraculous transformation and build a highly organized and coordinated network of 'Brain' consisting of over 30 billion nerve and neuron cells with precise planning and specialized development of a boney skeletal structure and various organs made of cells, tissues and muscles, essential to building an individual organism. Our neurons or nerve cells are formed simultaneously along with the formation and constitution of the brain in the very early months of embryonic development, almost parallel to the development of spinal cord or the spine as the very first structure of bones that is formed inside the womb after the sperm and egg cells fuse together to form a zygote. The heart is the next organ to get formed, which begins to beat in about three weeks into fetal life and even before, blood starts to pump through it. It brings out clearly, that contraction and relaxation is (or may be) essentially a voluntary characteristic of specific differentiated muscle cells of collagen proteins. And from here onward, the formation of everything else, body, limbs, other organs etc. take root. And by the time we are born, we will have as many as hundred billion neuron cells which we are going to essentially carry, without any replacement, for the rest of our life until death. Since the entire universe is electrical in nature and we make an integral part of this universe, our connection to the universal electric potential continuum or cosmic consciousness (a **de facto** *morphogenetic force field),* is most probably established, during this phase of fetus development itself and it is mediated first, through the spinal cord of the mother and independently after the moment the child inhales his first breath after birth and the umbilical cord is severed. But the infrastructure for an independent existence after birth is built-up and prepared for working during the development of the fetus into child, in the uterus itself. There is no experimental or instrumentally detected evidence for this kind of connection, so far, to the best of my knowledge. But, it seems that a conspicuous orientation of the head of embryo, fetus and the full grown baby-child, towards the tail end of the spinal cord (coccyx) of the mother / mulaadhar chakra during the period of her pregnancy, has something to do in establishing this connection with the universal electric potential continuum, **Figure-6 and Figure 7**. This seems logical in context of our prevalent belief that our connection to the universal consciousness is established through the *'Sahasradhar chakra'* / the Brain. The exact purpose and nature of such orientation of fetus to the close proximity of the region of the *'Muladhar Chakra'* of its mother is not clearly known, researched, discussed and described in literature on the subject. However, it is generally believed by the gynecologists that such orientation is meant for guiding the mature child for smooth delivery through the cervix into the birth canal. This may perhaps be another possible reason for such orientation, but the primary reason must be to keep the fetus child connected to the 'cosmic electric potential continuum' through the mother's brain to that of the fetus child. The other posterior, interior or the breech orientations of child within the uterus before delivery, are known to pose their own serious problems. I strongly feel, that the energy from the coccyx or the *'Muladhar Chakra'* of the mother might possibly be playing the role for the 'morphogenetic field forces' in assembling, shaping and replicating the formation of a miniature human body of a child, as per the genetic program encoded in the DNA of the fertilized female egg cell (zygote). And once the child is delivered and his umbilical cord is chopped, the child becomes an independent individual organism.

'Aiteryopanishad' (Upanishad) in its *Shlokas* 1 to 12 **(Figure 8 a & b)** also describes that the Paramatma / Prana / Consciousness enters a human body from the window in the middle of his brain. This window has been named as *'Vidruti'* alias *'Bramharandhra'* in Sanskrit and is the center of cosmic bliss. The Yogis are believed to concentrate their minds on this very spot during their meditation and enjoy the bliss of being in unison with the cosmic consciousness. The *'Bramharandhra'* window is not open for life time but only until a new born becomes independent individual with his / her first breath inhaled after the umbilical cord is severed after birth. *'Vidruti'* is the door used or is created by the cosmic consciousness at the time of conception and early development of the fetus for its entry through the nervous system of mother. Here lies therefore, the importance and reason for the orientation of the head of a developing fetus, towards the *'Muladhar chakra'* of the mother **(Figure 6)**. This *'Vidruti'* window, once closed after birth, breaks opens only from inside at the time of death when the finite locked consciousness (called *'Jeeva'*) within the body, exits and merges into its infinite source. Consciousness always remains active in the right eye (called the dream location), mind and heart in three states namely; awareness *(Jagruti),* dream *(Swapna)* and deep sleep *(Sushupti).* It may be noted here that 'finite, locked consciousness is not always lost through the *'Vidruti'* on death but exits mostly from several other locations. Only a true 'Yogi' who is able to exit his consciousness through *'Vidruti'* on his death is believed to have attained the coveted *'enlightenment'* or moksha. In modern scientific perspective, consciousness / cosmic electric charge / prana is carried by oxygen molecules, collected in lungs by means of

breathing, exchanged to the hemoglobin molecules in blood and pumped and reached to each and every cell of the human body through arteries, and tiny capillary veins by the heart.

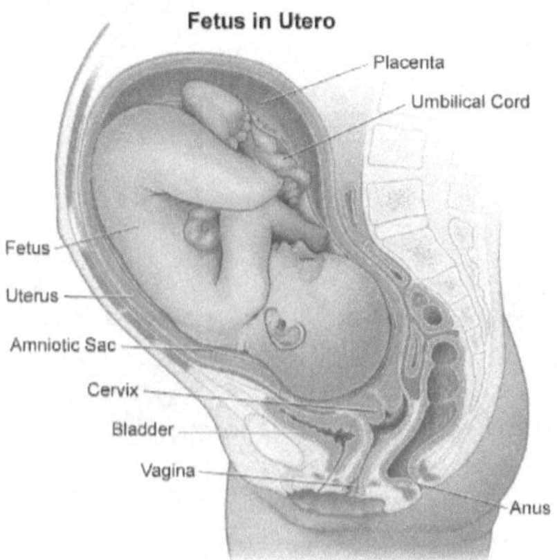

Figure 6. Orientation of the head of the fetus towards the cervix or Factually toward the energy grid- the *'Muladhar Chakra'* of its mother

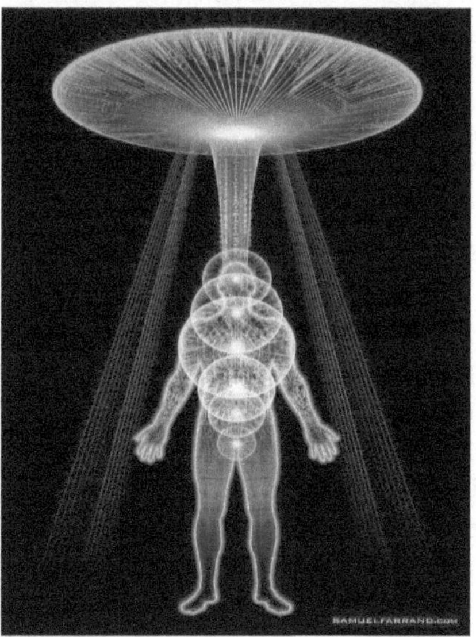

Figure 7. An artist's impression of our connection to the universal consciousness beginning from the Sahasradhar Chakra to the Muladhar in sequential order on the basis of our understanding from the Sanatan Vedic Philosophy and descriptions given by the enlightened Saints.

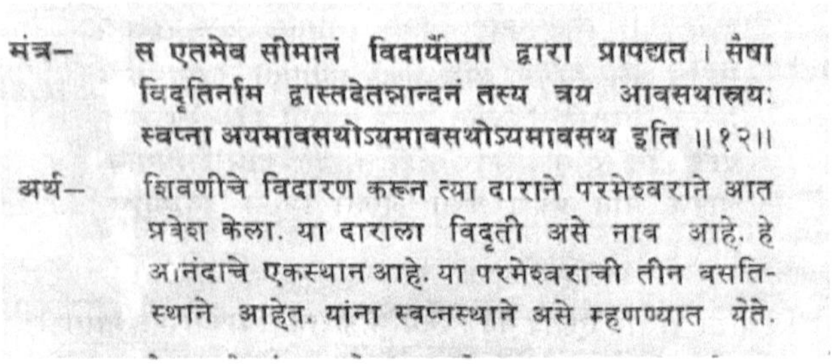

मंत्र— स एतमेव सीमानं विदार्यैतया द्वारा प्रापद्यत । सैषा
विदृतिर्नाम द्वास्तदेतन्नान्दनं तस्य त्रय आवसथास्त्रयः
स्वप्ना अयमावसथोऽयमावसथोऽयमावसथ इति ॥१२॥

अर्थ— शिवणीचे विदारण करून त्या दाराने परमेश्वराने आत
प्रवेश केला. या दाराला विदृती असे नाव आहे. हे
आनंदाचे एकस्थान आहे. या परमेश्वराची तीन वसति-
स्थाने आहेत. यांना स्वप्नस्थाने असे म्हणण्यात येते.

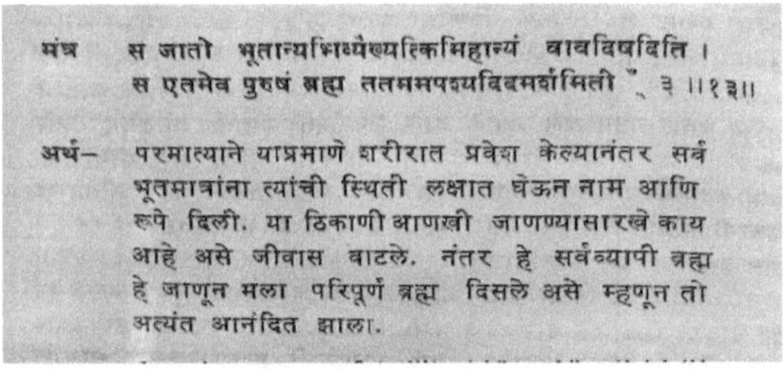

मंत्र— स जातो भूतान्यभिव्यैख्यत्किमिहान्यं वावदिषदिति ।
स एतमेव पुरुषं ब्रह्म ततममपश्यदिदमदर्शमिति ॥१३॥

अर्थ— परमात्याने याप्रमाणे शरीरात प्रवेश केल्यानंतर सर्व
भूतमात्रांना त्यांची स्थिती लक्षात घेऊन नाम आणि
रूपे दिली. या ठिकाणी आणखी जाणण्यासारखे काय
आहे असे जीवास वाटले. नंतर हे सर्वव्यापी ब्रह्म
हे जाणून मला परिपूर्ण ब्रह्म दिसले असे म्हणून तो
अत्यंत आनंदित झाला.

Figure 8 a & 8 b. The two Slokas from the '*Aiteryopanishad*' (Upanishad) that describe the way Prana / Consciousness / Parmatma enters the human fetus body with description in Marathi

The axons of the neuron cells from the developing brain, branch out within the entire matrix of the growing embryo. Neurons also project from the developing spinal cord and spread to the other areas of the body and nerves from the body project to the spinal cord. They conduct information between sense organs, the brain and other parts of the body in the form of electrical impulses that 'jump' between adjacent cells via gaps or synapses. The signals may pass by direct electrical connection, through intervening fluid or through chemical intermediaries called neurotransmitters. Neurons are typically bundled together with other cells and fatty, insulating tissue into nerves. The brain and the spinal cord form the central nervous system (CNS) of the human body. This interfaces through synapses with the peripheral nerve system in the skin, muscles and internal organs and is responsible for the continuous, involuntary processes such as, in regulating breathing and pulse rate of beating heart. The skull of the fetus baby remains very flexible so as to enable it to pass through the birth canal and opening through the cervix before birth. The skull cavity, enclosing the brain, gradually closes after birth and hardens with age.

Nikola Tesla, the renowned Serbian Physicist has appropriately described the interactions of environmental energies, forces and conditions with a new-born child as; "When a child is born its sense-organs are brought in contact with the outer *(that include terrestrial, planetary, galactic and universal)* world. The waves of sound, heat, and light beat upon its feeble body, its sensitive nerve-fibres quiver, the muscles contract and relax in obedience: a gasp, a breath, and in this act a marvelous little engine, of inconceivable delicacy and complexity of construction, unlike any on earth, is hitched to the wheel-work *(matter-energy re-cycling process)* of the Universe".

Unfortunately, a majority of people spend their life time without ever being aware, what a marvelous and complex body they possess and that they are surviving only at the mercy of the subtle and invisible terrestrial and universal forces. In fact, every living organism survives by fighting a continuous battle against ever changing environmental conditions by suitably adjusting the internal body metabolisms through release of specific enzymes through various endocrine and exocrine glands as a matter of its survival strategy. By the time the baby becomes an adult, the cell mass expands to over fifty (50) trillion, forming four characteristic types of basic tissues, namely; epithelial, connective, muscular and nervous, in addition to, a variety of their sub-tissues. All these specific cell-kinds have been grouped into some two hundred and fifty (250) different categories and they combine in turn, to construct nearly seventy eight (78) different organs of thirteen (13) major 'organ-systems', found in human bodies. These 'organ-systems' have been categorized in 'seven regional groupings' based on their locations within the body matrix, for the sake of convenience. Surprisingly, out of seventy eight (78) organs, only five (5), the heart, brain, lungs, kidneys and liver are considered to be very vital for a sustained life.

It has been estimated that about three hundred (300) million cells of our body die every minute and many of which are simply replaced through self-replication with our bodies being, individually programmed to precisely know which cells to replace, at what time, and how to do that. Each type of cell, therefore, has its own life expectancy, beyond which their continued functioning with efficiency becomes risky. On an average, barring a few cell types such as brain neuron, teeth enamel, and cells that make the 'Otic capsule', situated deep in the skull around the inner ear, almost all other body-cells are completely renewed every fifteen years. 'Vedic' philosophy, *'Kundalini Yog'* and spiritual practices from India, suggest that human body is connected to the universal cosmic consciousness *(Pran)* through the brain under the skull, and this connectivity, moves down along the spinal cord to the coccyx, the tail-end of the spinal cord. Although the concept of *'Kundalini'* does not formally constitute a part of curriculum in medical colleges, modern medical science admits, that the spinal cord is the most vital and crucial systemic part of the body. And yet, the literature on the integrated role of the spinal cord in explaining its cooperative and coordinated relationship with other vital systems *(respiratory, circulatory, digestive, metabolic, nervous, excretory, psycho-somatic and the mysterious 'Chakra' system)*, concerning the flow of universal cosmic energy, functioning of the neuron-network and physiological, metabolic, biochemical and sympathetic psycho-behavioral responses of the body as a conscious organism, is not clearly known in a holistic way. The available literature on this subject, though scholarly and insightful in content, continues to be routine, stereo-type and hazy descriptions for several decades, either because of the complexity of the problem, paucity of new original research data or inadequacy of appropriate words for writing a clear perceptive description and interpretation. Besides, there is no precise understanding on the factual physical existence of the *'chakras'* and their influence in the working of various secretary glands of human body, in relation to comprehensive understanding of medical-human-anatomy, genetics, physiology, metabolic biochemistry, psycho-physical behavior, functional disorders of organs, health, nutrition and diseases, in an integrated way. In general, the concept of *'Chakras'*, their descriptions, appeal, experience and acceptance of their role in human life, continues to remain clouded in mystery, subjective, symbolic and purely metaphysical in the discipline of Yoga science. I must admit here, that based on the belief in the existence of *chakras* as the given truth, some very beautiful, insightful, innovative and apparently realistic images have been drawn by very talented and innovative artists to help any viewer in forming a mental perception about them. And yet, their formal existential acceptance and integration with modern education in medical sciences, at the global level, is far away from a global concurrence. The very fact, that the concept of *'chakras'* has remained in the literature on Yoga and in the heart of yoga practitioners for thousands of years, suggests that practicing 'chakra *meditation'* may indeed be providing some kind of psychic, mentally perceptible or emotionally felt, sensory experience of a specific energy-matter interaction. The whole concept of *'chakras'* and circulation of the universal conscious energy *(Prana)* through them appears to be connected to some kind of invisible but structurally laid, in-built ion channels. Voluntary efforts of several courageous medical specialists around the world in cooperation of practicing yoga specialists, subjecting themselves for experimentation, instrumental observation and detection of changes in their body during practice of their 'chakra meditation', are closing the gaps about the likely connection between the 'chakras' and working of human brain. Still, however, there is much more to achieve before the relationship is universally accepted. Perhaps, with recognition, acceptance and observation of the 'International day of Yoga' every year by the world since 2015, this apprehensive seclusion, with more intensive research done, may break the ice forever. My own doubt is that we have not yet understood the factual scientific meaning of the word 'Chakras" in relation to the flow of energy within the human body and their bearing on the physical, physiological, metabolic, psychic and behavioral working of human being as an organism. I have identified several glaring contradictions mentioned in books by celebrated authors, which have gone into multiple editions for several years. Some examples being; energy *(Prana)* flows from the lower most *Muladhar Chakra* to the top *Sahasrasar Chakra*; Energy *(Prana)* flows upward from the Muladhar chakra through Ida and *Pingala nadis* and so also through the Sushumna nadi but meet themselves in the top *Sahasrasar chaka* (Crown chakra). This description seems to be considerably misleading. Particularly, when the source of universal electric energy potential continuum percolates from top of the atmospheric layer towards the surface of the Earth, and human brain neuron cells to be sending electrical signals down to the entire matrix of the body, flow of energy from bottom to the top through the three *nadi* channels does not appear to be logical. There is no clear discrimination between the nature of energy, flowing through both these systems. And if they essentially refer to the same kind of energy, then there is certainly a misconception or deep gap in our understanding about the directions of flow of universal cosmic energy through the body system.

Here, as I look at the problem, I foresee three distinct energy flowing systems within human body. And they are; (1) Respiratory, blood circulatory, endocrine glandular, digestive, excretory and brain central nervous systems (CNS) to be forming a composite integrated system (2) *Ida, Pingala and Sushumna Nadis* along with the peripheral nervous system (PNS) forming the second energy flowing system and (3) the chakras, universal cosmic energy potential continuum, the muscular network with skeletal bone structure and the exocrine glandular network to be forming their integrated third system for flow of energy within the body matrix.

I will attempt to logically explain these three energy systems the way I perceive in my attempt to remove the confusion prevalent in the literature.

As it appears, from the literature, the spinal-cord as a systemic infrastructure of the human body constitutes a composite of several separate systems of energy channels, which simultaneously work in co-operation with each other. These channels are; (1) the bundle of neuron cells from the brain, constituting the network of sensory nervous system and neuron network (2) The blood circulatory system consisting of arteries, veins and capillaries (3) the executive and physiology-regulatory endocrine glandular channel, mutually connected by means of ducts to the blood circulating arteries, veins and capillaries (4) the exocrine glandular and muscular network within the matrix of body and bones, operating the various organs and bone-joints, helping in motivation (5) the channel of seven energy power-grids called the 'Chakras' and (6) The popular metaphysical concept of the three 'Nadis" known as; the Ida, the *Pingala* and the *Sushumna,* believed to be responsible for the flow of universal cosmic consciousness within the human body. All these six channels extend from the brain inside the skull and run up to the perineurium of the gilial cells of the spinal cord in case of male and up to the cervix in case of females, where the so called *'Muladhar Chakra'* is believed to be respectively located.

In Hatha Yoga, the spinal cord (spine) is considered to be the center of our sacred anatomy and the microcosm of the 'Axis Mundi', i.e. the pillar energy axis between cosmic Heaven and Earth that supports the Earth as a living entity. This pillar axis, which paradoxically remains in constant motion, factually remains motionless at the center. The spinal cord also carries a bundle of sensory nerve (neuron) cells from the brain to the tail end-bone of spinal cord, the coccyx. These nerve cells are distributed within the matrix of the body with their sensory tips ending into the hypodermis layer, below the outer epidermal skin, **Figure 9.**

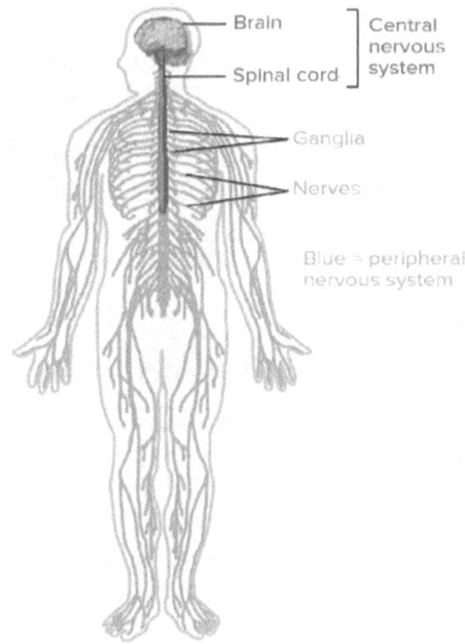

Figure 9. Diagramatic representation of the human nervous system

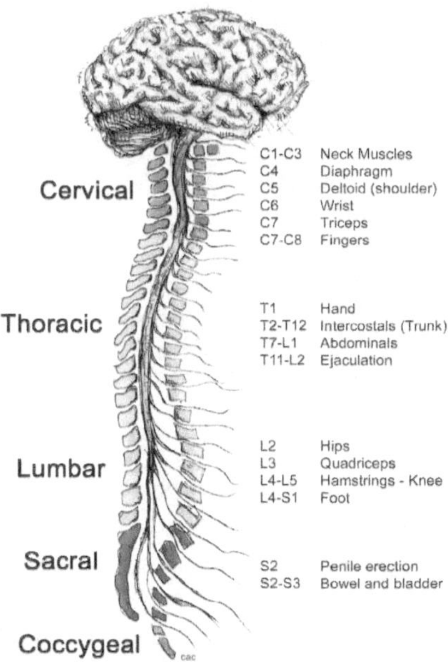

Figure 10. Structure of the Spinal Cord and Regions of nerves that control the working of various organs and parts of body

Specialized neurons carry messages from the skin, muscles, joints, and internal organs to the spinal cord about pain, temperature, touch, vibration, and proprioception. These messages are then relayed to the brain along one of two pathways: the *spinothalmic* tract and the *lemniscal* pathway. These pathways are in different locations in the spinal cord, so an injury might not affect them in the same way or to the same degree.

Each segment of the spinal cord receives sensory input from a particular region of the body. Scientists have mapped these areas and determined the "receptive" fields for each level of the spinal cord. *Neighboring fields overlap each other, so the lines on the diagram are approximate.*

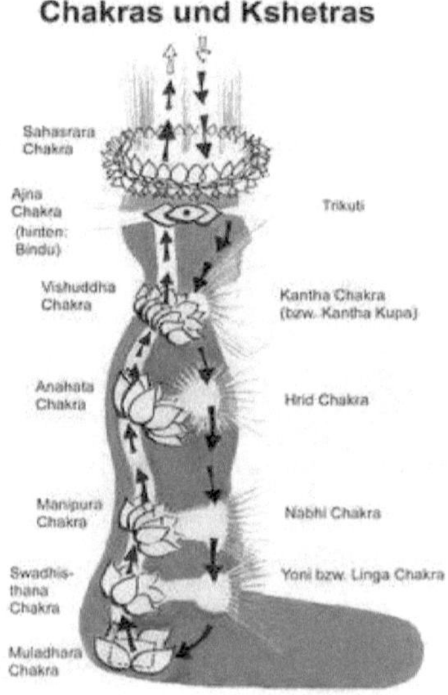

Figure 11. The Chakras and their corresponding locations in human body

The functions and operation of various organs of the body, constituting the essential components of respiratory, circulatory, digestive, metabolic, psycho-physiological, excretory and mind-memory systems for survival as an independent organism, are controlled by the muscular contraction and relaxation, as per the commands received from the brain, which constantly analyses the signals received from neural axons and their complex assembly junctions within the body matrix, interacting continually with the external epigenetic and morphogenetic environment.

In this respect the entire skin of human body acts like a sensor in transmitting information about external environment to the brain.

The seven nodal power grids called the 'Chakras' that lay distributed along the spinal cord, mutually connect sequentially with the universal electric potential energy continuum /cosmic consciousness by means of three channels called–'Nadis'. *Nadi* essentially means a flowing river. And in the sense of its meaning the Nadis connecting the Chakras with universal electric energy potential continuum actually flow electric current down the gradient. These three *'Nadis'*, are known by the names as the 'Ida', *'Pingala'* and the *'Sushumna'* as part of the system that circulates the universal energy inside the body. Although, it is not very clear, but it logically appears, that the chakras along with these three *nadis,* constitute a separate system from the bundle of neuron cell axons from the brain and distributed within the body through the spinal cord, **Figure 10**.

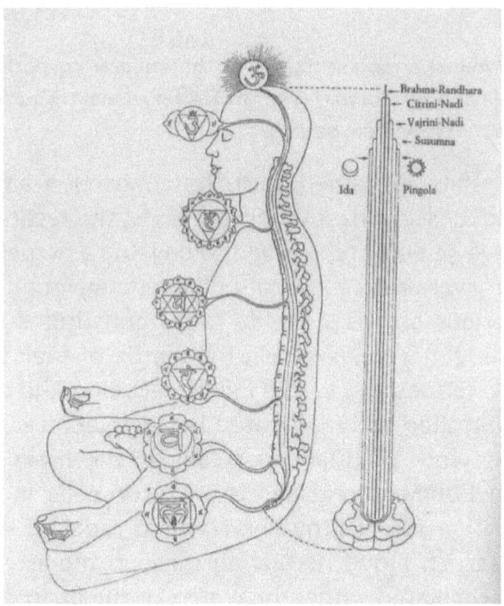

Figure 12. The Ida, Pingala and the Sushumna Nadis

Before I go over to explaining the *Nadis,* it would be worthwhile to know that all the living organisms on the Earth depend on the Sun for their survival. Whereas the only satellite of Earth, the Moon is solely responsible for retention of the Earth's atmosphere.

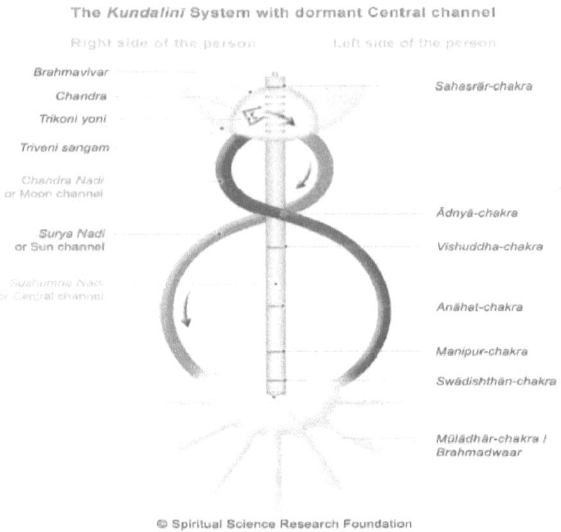

Figure 13. A diagrammatic representation of the integral connection of the three Nadis *(Ida, Pingala and Sushumna)* with the Universal electric potential continuum *(Cosmic consciousness)* and the seven Chakras

Whereas the first is concerned with the connection and flow of the universal cosmic consciousness within the body, the second is essentially meant to perceive self-awareness and to develop a perpetually dynamic strategy for survival under external epigenetic environment. The flow of energy to various organs in all life forms constitutes the movement of atomic ions and molecules within the matrix of their bodies, across cell membranes, tissues and within individual cells. And this movement of energy is controlled and moderated by the electrical activity within the neuronal network of trillions of cells in the brain **(Figures-9)** in response to environment outside. The neuron cells in human brains draw their nutrition for healthy survival and required electric energy from the oxygen rich blood circulating through the arteries and veins distributed and circulated within the matrix of the brain, by the heart. A gradient of electric potential difference is always generated, maintained and regulated through a complex biochemical synthesis and release of various proteins and enzymes, by the cellular cytoplasmic factories and membranes in response to the epigenetic environment outside, which is sensed by the receptor axons of the neuron cells embedded within layers of dermis and hypodermis below the epidermal skin of bodies of all living organisms. It is not clear if the energy component of the universal electric potential continuum and the so called 'Morphogenetic energy fields' proposed by the British Scientist Rupert Sheldrake are essentially the same?

Every material thing (living and non-living) existing in the universe is made of atoms, which are the primary units of elements. And there are only 118 kinds of elements in the universe, known so far, which have been ingeniously classified into a table, on the basis of the periodic similarities of physical and chemical properties, when arranged in order of their increasing atomic numbers **(Figure-14)**.

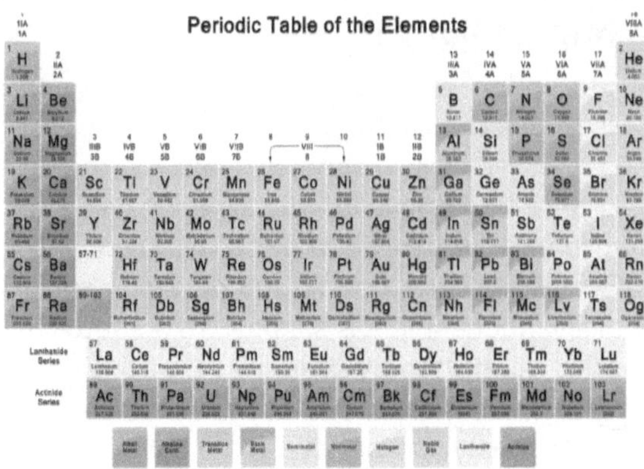

Figure 14. The Periodic Table of elements

Every material object is created by a specific combination of one or more than one kind of these element atoms. The stability of individual atoms and those of a multitude of their combinations into structures of various kinds are governed by four kinds of natural forces namely; weak interaction, strong interaction, electromagnetic and gravitation. All molecular structures are formed by a combination of similar or dissimilar element atoms by transfer or sharing of negatively charged electrons with each other, under certain set of conditions. These molecular structures disintegrate into their component atoms with even slightest change of conditions under which they were formed. The atoms, so falling apart, are re-cycled for the creation of similar or different kind of structures. Perpetual re-cycling of atomic elements in this way is the fundamental law of nature. And during such re-cycling processes, the elemental atoms (except in case of nuclear disintegration) retain and maintain their individual identities as to who they are, their characteristics and properties. It may be emphasized, that because atoms combine with similar or dissimilar atoms by exchange or sharing of their negatively charged electrons with each other, electric charge is therefore the primary cause for creation of all the molecular and material structures and so also for their disintegration. In short, it is the electric charge that drives the creation of material world in the universe and that includes both the living and the non-living or the conscious and unconscious kinds.

Universal electric potential continuum and *in-vivo* building of a human body form

Ever since the conception as a fertilized ovule takes place, a human zygotic fetus gets connected to the universal consciousness from within the womb of its mother. This connection allows the fetus to grow in morphology, size and shape with the help of universal, terrestrial, epigenetic and morphogenetic forces that come into play, beginning with the formation of limbs and feet first to the development of head in the last. The nutrients and nourishment is supplied to the fetus from the blood plasma of the mother connected by an umbilical cord. Why I say that this should be the order or sequence in development of the fetus is from the observation and analogously similar developmental processes in the plant kingdom. The fruits develop in general to higher maturity at the far end of the connecting stem with the plant or tree from which the fruit draws its supply of nutrition and energy. This may perhaps also be the reason, why the head of the developing fetus remains oriented towards the base chakra (the '*Muladhar Chakra*') of its mother during the entire period of gestation (**Figure-5 and 6**), because every human being, irrespective of gender remains continuously connected to the universal cosmic consciousness from the side of its head and internally meet in the nasal cavity or possibly in the lungs, the doorways through which we inhale our life-giving oxygen gas from the atmosphere. Hemoglobin in blood, pick up these Oxygen molecules which in turn, deliver energy to cellular tissues by exchanging the negatively charged electrons, maintaining thereby a gradient of electric potential across the body matrix. It may be interesting to note, why there appears to be a significant correlation of the orientation of the head of fetus in uterus, towards the coccyx bone of the mother. It is well known that the upper portion of the skull cavity of the child within uterus is the last to develop and finally close, much after its birth.

In attempts to suitably explain the intimate connection of the human beings and all other forms of animal organisms on the Earth to the best possible extent, the essential message about the enigmatic concepts of 'Soul' in contrast to the perceptions we have been holding dear in our minds for thousands of years as our 'inherited-given-for-granted cultural or traditional truth'. In doing so, I have with due apology picked up, adopted and modified the beautiful X-Ray like image of a seated human being in meditative posture from the public domain (From the website of 'Pinterest' under their provision and policy of permitting use and reproduction of pictures / photographs from their site for 'Fair Use') available on the internet **(Figure-15)**. I have modified this picture with superimposition of some changes that I personally feel convey the basic concepts of the message attempted to be conveyed through these two books ('A Scientific Look at the Concept of Soul: An Attempted Synthesis', Zorba Books, 2017 and 'A Scientific Look at the Concepts of Soul, Rebirth, Work and the Law of Karma: An Attempted Synthesis', Zorba Books, 2019. And with reference to this picture,

Figure 15. A representative diagrammatic picture of a human being in relation to the universal electric energy continuum and the internal power grids (Chakras) that exercise control over the functions of various organs of the human body in coordination with its control system within the brain.

I attribute the circular aura around the human head, marked with positive (+) signs to represent the all-pervading, omnipresent, universal cosmic electric charge potential continuum, which connects the human bodies from the top end of the head and is regulated in bodies of human and all other life-forms by means of the ionic currents with bodies continually remaining in connection to this source of energy from the moment of conception and birth to the last breath at death. The nodal power grids *(known as the Chakras)* administer and control the flow of the ionic currents to the various organs which constitute the integral parts of our respiratory, digestive, thought, physiology and excretory systems, and help us in continuously consuming and dissipating energy (Entropy) to stay biologically conscious and living. These organs are operated by the muscles made of fibrous collagen proteins that contract and relax with exchange of atomic ions and consequently the electric charges across them. In short, the whole body constitutes a self-automated electric machine that works on the exchange and power of ionic electric current. The two elliptical electron orbital rings in the picture around the lungs and heart region, corresponding to the *'Anahat Chakra'* represent, that it is here the principal currency of life i.e. the oxygen molecules exchange electric charges to the iron-rich hemoglobin molecules of blood, which are pumped and reached to every nook and corner of the body through the cascading arteries, veins, capillaries and vesicles, which criss-cross the entire matrix of the body matter. Astrophysicists declare that electric charges, proliferate the entire universe and the universe in factual realty is essentially electric in nature. The depiction of this picture, therefore drives home the point that what we call a 'Soul' which is traditionally believed to make and drive us around at will as a 'conscious organism', is fundamentally nothing else but only the electric charge. And this charge is universally quantized and conserved, does not change in value, nature and characteristics. It is omni-present and is the primary cause for the formation of material structures. It fosters linkages and bonds with atoms of other kinds to form complex assemblies, associations, enables motivation and is also the root cause for disintegration and destruction of material structures. These functional attributes of the 'electric charge' are essentially the same what have been traditionally attributed to the functioning of the enigmatic 'Soul' for thousands of years. Moreover, electric charge being universally quantized and similar everywhere, it justifies the Vedic statement- "what is present in the universe, the same exists within the body of all living organisms" or in other words 'what drives the universe also drives all the living organisms including the vegetative world". What intrigues me most being the fact that the plant world should be resting on the surface of the Earth with their 'brainy root-tips' lying buried upside-down in contrast to the animal world. The trees not only think critically and respond to the environment demands and insect-pest attack but also give their helping hand to other species of trees and insects, if needed for their survival and alternately seek their help for its own protection ('The Hidden Life of Trees: What the Feel, How They Communicate: Discoveries from a Secret -World' By Peter Wohlleben, William Collins, 2017 (Figure-13). Origin and birth of a new life-form in general and human being in particular has been beautifully described by Nikola Tesla in his write-up –'**Unlock the Universe With-in-Yourself'** and his words are worth quoting here, essentially to demonstrate how electric charges in the form of ionic current is intimately connected with the process of new creation; "when a child is born its sense-organs are brought in contact with the outer world. The waves of sound, heat, and light beat upon its feeble body, its sensitive nerve-fibres quiver, the muscles contract and relax in obedience: a gasp, a breath, and in this act a marvelous little engine, of inconceivable delicacy and complexity of construction, unlike any on earth, is hitched to the wheel-work of the Universe (the universal electric potential continuum in perpetually dynamic state of creation and destruction).

With this, I wish to end this article here with the hope that my enlightened readers would appreciate my attempt to deal with this extremely complex subject in connecting our ancient *'Sanatan Vedic'* concepts with modern scientific understanding.

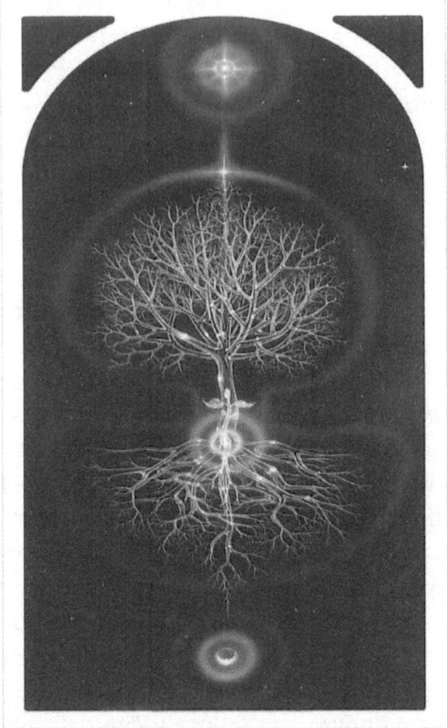

Figure 16. Upside-Down orientation of the roots of trees and plants below the surface of the Earth

Acknowledgement

I wish to acknowledge my sincere thanks and gratitude for taking their valuable time to go through this lengthy manuscript and considerable input, feedback, appreciation and encouragement received from renowned specialists; Dr. Dattatreya G. Mhaskar and Dr. Balkrishna G. Matapurkar. But for their help, I would not have dared to write it.

CHAPTER – 9

The Twenty One Attributes of Parmatma / GOD

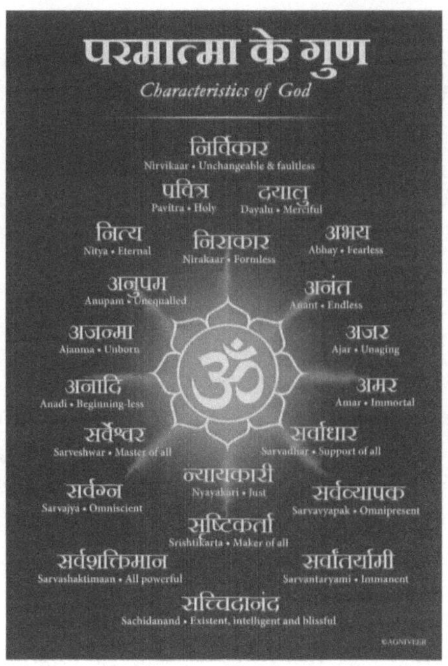

This beautiful picture, summarizing the twenty one attributes, that human beings have been ascribing to the creator of the universe called the 'Parmatma', has suddenly caught my attention and while attempting to compare and correlate these attributes in identifying a suitable candidate from amongst the currently known natural entities, constituting the structure of matter, unrivalled by modern physicists, the following short write up has sprouted from my mind. And I have pleasure in sharing it for wider discussion and critical analysis to the enlightened people as a sincere attempt to give meaning and to revalidate our ancient conceptual entities in the light of new knowledge and modern scientific understanding. Hope, people would appreciate and enjoy reading this.

"All the Twenty One Attributes, mentioned in the above picture ascribed to the 'PARAMATMA'- the 'Universal Soul' or 'Universal Consciousness' and synonymously to the 'GOD', if critically and analytically considered, logically discussed and philosophically thought over and compared, are equally applicable to the negatively charged fundamental particle of nature-The 'ELECTRON'. 'The Electron' is known to be an indestructible particle of nature and its life has been estimated to be 10^{66} Years, which is more than the life of the universe itself. Moreover, 'Electron' is a common constituent of all matters, universally distributed, quantized in its value of electric charge and mass, creates and breaks almost all material structures in nature from the elementary units of matter the atoms. Besides being universally 'entangled', electrons remain indistinguishable from one another from any corner of the universe. And factually according to the scientist James Morgia, "The Mighty Electron Recycles All" and makes and breaks all creations in the universe".

"Electricity is everywhere, even in the human body. Defining what is meant by electricity, depends on who is providing the definition. Physicists and mathematicians define it in one way whereas, a man on the street defines it in another. Piezoelectricity, thermoelectricity and bioelectricity are all forms of electricity. In a similar vein, "Heat" as an energy, has several modes for its movements: conduction, radiation, convection etc. It may be remembered here that, though "Heat" is a form of energy, electricity is not. Analogically, a flood of molten lava is not a flow of heat nor is an electric current but a river of electricity. Electricity is a fundamental quality of matter and therefore is used to characterize other things. Electricity as the flow of electric charge travels through a circuit when there is sufficient voltage difference to push it along the wires. It moves slowly. On the contrary, electromagnetic energy flows only in one direction at near the speed of light from the source to the load and comes out of the circuit as light or heat, never to return. However, electric charge is conserved in the circuit and it cannot be created or destroyed but only moved from place to place. Electric current is measured in Coulombs per second (Amperes) while electromagnetic energy is measured in Joules. There is no way to convert one to another as they are unrelated. Whereas, electric current is matter (charged particles) electromagnetism is energy (S. S. Chirott; thunderbolts.info/wp/2024/04/24/what-is-electricity-5/)"

In fact the whole universe is now known to be electrical in nature. Our cells are specialized to conduct electrical currents. Electricity is required for the nervous system to send signals throughout the body and to the brain, making it possible for us to move, think and feel our everyday experiences. I therefore, consider, 'Electron and its electric charge' to be *de facto* the most 'enigmatic entity' to humanity, almost synonymously but differently called by the names as; 'I or Me' / Self / Soul /Psyche / Astral Body / Atma, Jeevatma / Paramatma / Conscience / Subtle Body / Spirit / Spiriton / Subconscious / Super-conscious / Voice of the Heart / Energy- informational matrix / Reactive Mind or a Quantum Monod etc. in essentially describing the same thing popularly known since antiquity as the Soul". It is worth standing away from the maddening crowd and orthodox views, pause for a while and introspect to see if the burden of several of our ancient concepts that we have been carrying with us since time immemorial, can be physically defined, have any credibility, continued relevance or correlation with any of the several components of matter unravelled by modern scientists and our continued efforts to realize and understand the enigmatic 'Soul' as perceived since antiquity, is only a matter of the 'Proverbial Chase for the non-existent wild goose'.

References:

1. 'A Scientific Look at the Concepts of Soul, Rebirth, Work and the Law of Karma: An Attempted Synthesis' by Anil Vishnu Moharir, 2019, Zorba Books, Paperback, pp 136, ISBN 978-93-88497-84-8 And

2. 'Mighty Electron Recycles All' by James Morgia, Trafford Publishing, pp 98, ISBN 1-55212-717-6.

3. 'Elemente der Physhophysik' By Gustav T. Fechner (1860) Breitkopf und Hartel, Liepzig, Germany.

4. 'Nature from Within: Gustav Theodore Fechner and his psychophysical worldviews (C. Klohr. Trans.) (2004) University of Pittsburgh Press' Article by By M. Heidelberger in Fox, C.R. (2020) Gustav Fechner: The

5. Man who introduced Soul to science, Academia Letters, Artcle 38, https://doi.org/10.20935/AL38.December 2020.

6. What is Electricity

7. S. S. Chiirott; thunderbolts.info/wp/2024/04/24/what-is- electricity-5/ Dated 29-04-2024). Original Post April 24, 2014.

CHAPTER – 10

Work, its Origin, Kinds and the Law of Karma: A Synthesis of their Scientific Foundation and Obligations for Human Survival

Abstract

This article traces the definition and origin of perpetual work in the creation of the universe and it's various kinds in relation to the conscious life forms and human beings in particular. The origin and operation of the Universal Law of Karma has been explained on the basis of physics and modern molecular genetics. The recently discovered, perpetually ongoing process of DNA- methylation in all living organisms, which essentially defines the strategy mechanism adopted by the organism for survival under continuously changing epigenetic environmental (which include physical, physiological, terrestrial, atmospheric, cosmic and universal) conditions, has been functionally associated with the ancient, invisible mythological character called the **'Chitragupta'** since the Vedic period in India. The personified 'Chitragupta', as an assistant of Yamaraj, the deity of death, has been believed to be secretly writing detailed **'Record of all the Work Done by the Living Organism in its whole life'.** What seems astonishingly marvelous is, how the 'Rishis' from the 'Vedic Period' in India could know the subtlest function and role of the DNA molecules and their *–methylation* process as a strategy for survival by the organism under changing epigenetic environment? The ancient personified 'Chitragupta' is therefore not a myth or a concept of blind faith but a physical scientific truth. The beautiful parallel of the process of DNA-methylation, drawn in this article with the character of 'Chitragupta' who resides secretly unseen within every individual cell of the body and ceaselessly records the history of all interactions of the organism with epigenetic environment from the moment of its conception, development, birth to death, appears to be fascinating and amazingly interesting. How I wish the scientists today to look to the Vedic Philosophy from the point of view of modern science.

Introduction

Why there is perpetual work in nature?

The Universe is known to be filled with only energy and matter of various kinds, controlled by four types of natural forces, known to a physicist as; 'Weak interaction', 'Strong interaction', 'Electromagnetic' and 'Gravitation'.[1-3] Whereas only one tenth of the total matter present in the universe is visible to human eye, the balance nine tenth, continues to remain occluded and is called the dark matter or dark energy. The nature, manifestation, spread or distribution and properties of dark energy and its transformation into visible matter, continue to be a great mystery, despite tremendous progress in cosmological sciences and attempts to explain all the four natural forces by one single theory (Standard Model).[4-6] The perpetual interplay of the conversion of dark energy into visible matter and its recycling back into energy is the fundamental law of Nature. According to the modern concepts of cosmology, a Universe is believed to contain a cluster of about one hundred billion galaxies, with each galaxy consisting of about one hundred billion individual stars. And it is estimated that over a fifty orders of magnitude of this universe, lies beyond the farthest universe, visibly seen with help of most powerful telescopes located on Earth and those positioned at 540 Km above sea level in geo-stationary orbit in space, the Hubble Space Telescope.[3-7] Light energy at its velocity of **1,86,000 miles per second** or **2,99,792.458 Km per second,** would require at least a million years to diagonally travel across any single galaxy from its one end to the other. Recent evidence gathered by the National Aeronautics and Space Administration (NASA), USA suggests that the cluster of stars within individual galaxies and galaxies across multitude of universes are not individually isolated but are mutually interconnected. **Figure 1[4] and 2** below, depict the limits of the extent of universal matter from its microscopic to the macroscopic dimensions and the physical equipments that have helped man to unfold these limits, which extend from 10^{-30} **to** 10^{+45} **cm.** These seemingly extreme limits also represent, the extent and dimensions of human knowledge today and the human brain and mind are not only concerned with everything that lies, within these limits but are perpetually attempting to comprehend and correlate his own existence in relation to them.[1-7] However, it is clear that the key to the presence of a variety of compound matter present in the universe is the formation and availability of the lightest element i.e. Hydrogen atoms (protons) in abundance and their fusion into the formation of the other fundamental elemental atomic unit matter of about 118 different kinds, each with an individually unique mass as well as chemical, structural and physical properties.[2] And each kind of these elemental atoms, were formed in the nuclear furnaces during the formation of Stars after the singularity exploded with a 'Big Bang', approximately 14 billion years ago.[6,7] Accurate observations made with the help of the most advanced telescopes reveal that an exact balance exists between the positive energy of matter that formed and the negative energy of gravitation that immediately comes into play so that no net energy is actually required for creation of the rest of the universe.

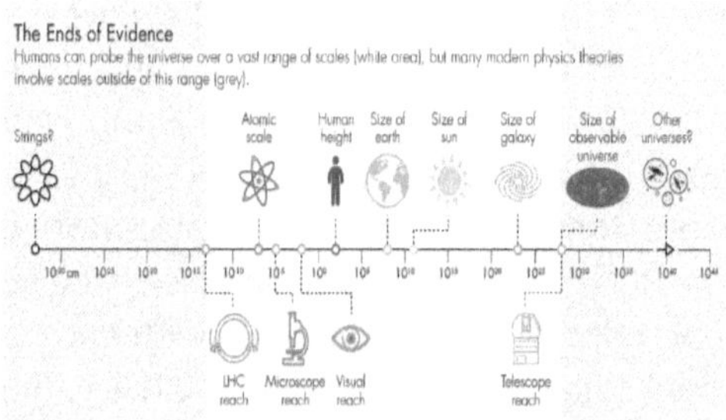

Figure 1. Dimensional limits of the extent of material and energy continuum of the universe and corresponding human knowledge today (*Reproduced with apologies from an unidentified source*).

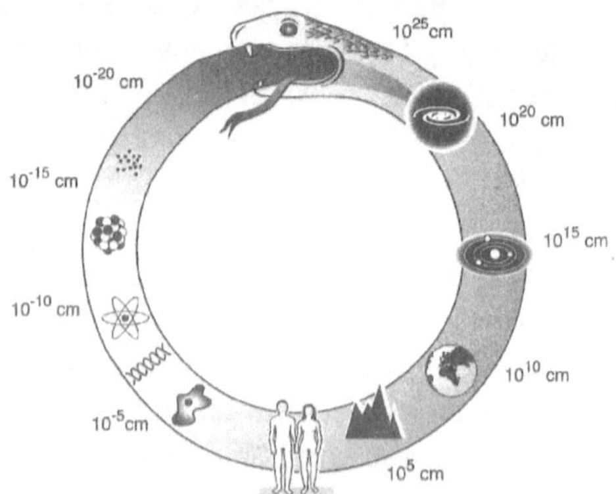

Figure 2. The ORABORUS. Indicating the connecting links between the micro-world of particles, nuclei and atoms (left) and the cosmos (right). *Reproduced here, with apology from the book–'Just Six Numbers', by Martin Rees, Phoenix (1999).[4]* The illustration, as I consider, is also the pictorial representation of the factual, fundamental, Universal law of perpetual recycling of energy into matter and vice-versa in both, the inanimate (inert) and animate (living) forms of matter in nature.

A cyclic inter-play in creation of both inanimate and animate matter and their subsequent disintegration into basic building blocks of the elemental atomic matter from which they were formed and later it's annihilation with release of considerable amounts of energy under the action of the four kinds of known forces of nature, has become the sine qua non (acquired attribute) of the manifestation of nature with all its spectacular grandeur and beauty. However,

where and how, the all-pervading 'consciousness' and awareness about self- existence fits into this scheme of universal creation is still a mystery and the source for speculation, theories and debate. Many thinkers believe that 'Consciousness' may be the fifth force of nature but the scientists are reluctant to admit so. The other probability that has been put forward is that 'consciousness' may be a hitherto unknown and most possibly an unrecognized, collective attribute of the quantized negative or positive electric charges respectively on an electron and a proton, as a manifestation of the primordial elemental matter or energy itself. Quantized units of electric charges (on an electron or a proton) is also fundamental to both the creation and destruction of elemental matter as well as to structures of more complex nature arising out of a combination of different atoms and molecules. The life of an electron has been estimated to be 10^{66} years and is perhaps the most stable of all the elementary particles known to human beings. It may be curious to argue whether 'consciousness' exists or does not exist, at the sub-structural level (Quarks) of proton or electron and other elementary nuclear particles with fractional electric charges on them? And billions of years after his appearance on the Earth, man is still searching for scientific answers about his own consciousness, his origin, the purpose and time span of his existence. Despite these limitations, what is most evident is; that creation of matter (inanimate and animate) its sustenance for a specific predetermined period of time and its subsequent annihilation has evolved itself into a continually rhythmic, dynamic process, marked by an equilibrium in periodic cycles of energy consumption, transformation and work done against the forces of nature. Obviously therefore, performing work and accumulating that continuously in building up the potential energy has become an acquired- perpetual characteristic process in nature. Nothing can ever remain without action / work even for a fraction of a second and every inanimate and animate matter is helplessly driven to remain at work by way of its inherent qualities and natural tendencies. Whereas, progressive accumulation of potential energy, beyond limits of sustenance leads to disaster, destruction or annihilation, progressive shedding of potential energy (through personal sacrifice / inaction) leads back towards the origin and source of primordial energy or the source of consciousness.[8-14] Therefore, it is probable that a 'stimulation / initiation of some kind' similar to 'desire or urge in man' on behalf of a hitherto unknown kind of a primordial 'Force of nature' must have set the first action of transforming the abundant dark-energy into visible matter and push it into action for performing ceaseless work. The three of the four forces of nature, namely; weak interaction, strong interaction and electromagnetic, as described above, perhaps come into play, during and after the matter in its stable element form is actually created. And with the creation of mass, follows the force of gravitation. However, though difficult, the origin of the force of 'strong interaction' which binds the sub-nuclear particles together may be resulting from the stimulus received from the hitherto unknown 'Force of Nature' that provides mass to energy. The weak and strong interactive forces within the nucleus of every atom of various elements compete with the electromagnetic force for ultimate control over the atom. At times, when the strong force wins, protons and neutrons get strongly bound to produce a stable atom and when the electromagnetic force wins, it leads to an unstable entity with production of a variety of disintegrating radio- active nuclei. The Yang-Mills equation, credited to Robert Lawrence Mills and Chen Ning Yang explained the puzzling properties of subatomic particles on the basis of difference between left and right spin, when particles interact through the weak force. **Whereas electric charge is a source of an electromagnetic field, the electromagnetic field itself is not the source of an electric charge.** Electromagnetism also does not change electric charges and the field is a source for itself by itself. Electrons were created at the time the Big Bang occurred, around 13.8 billion years ago, as energized photons interacted with each other to create an electron-positron pair. In fact, electrons are created from quarks (a fundamental sub-atomic particle). A quark is a tiny particle which makes up protons and neutrons. Atoms, in turn are made of protons, neutrons and electrons. It was once thought that all three of those were fundamental particles, which cannot be broken up into anything smaller.

Unfortunately, neither the sequence, order and process involved in the creation of electrons, protons and neutrons and assembly of nuclei of various element atoms nor the sequence in the hierarchy involved amongst the four 'forces of nature' is scientifically known to mankind. The experiments conducted with powerful atom smashing machines- the particle accelerators, have only revealed the presence of various constituent elementary particles, involved in their composition, assembly and as components but not about the process of their creation. And as long as such stimulation and recycling in converting dark energy into matter and vice versa exist, so long the perpetual performance of work (in the form of the cycle of creation and destruction) will not be over. And this cycle of creation and destruction is common to both the inanimate and animate matter because they both originate and constitute the same primordial elemental atomic material in their systems. Ever since the element atoms of 118 kinds were created at the beginning of the universe about 13.8 billion years ago, they have remained so and retained their individual identities and characteristic physical and chemical properties. In other word, all these individual element atoms of 118 kinds are the physical material entities that are conscious of their own existence, identity, capacity and properties. And since the basic element atoms are themselves being the conscious entities, a profound question that arises being; Is 'consciousness' in a living being, including humans, an attribute of collective consciousness of the billions of atoms that constitute the body parts and their mechanism?

Merging boundaries of physics, physical chemistry and biochemistry of matter

Rupert Sheldrake [15] has recently come out with his revolutionary new concept and 'Hypothesis of Formative Causation' which states that the forms of self- organizing systems are shaped by morphic fields. Morphic fields organize atoms, molecules, crystals, organelles, cells, tissues, organs, organisms, communities, societies, ecosystems, planetary systems, solar systems and galaxies at all imaginable complexities. These morphic fields also contain an inherent memory given by the process and frequencies of morphic resonance culminating in providing each and every kind of thing a 'collective memory'. Thus, morphic fields that shape the growing biological organisms are called morphogenetic fields, in social organization they can be called social fields; and in organization of the mental activity- the mental fields. And all such kinds of fields are shaped, stabilized and act on materials to put them into perpetual work through morphic resonance. Innumerable reports from National Aeronautics And Space Administration (NASA) -USA indicate the presence of perpetual, strong geo-magnetic fields around the Earth and when a big storm of solar plasma, originating from the coronal mass ejection from the Sun, force waves of intense ionization rippling through the Earth's upper atmosphere, they cause electric currents to flow through the topsoil and shake the entire magnetic field of the planet Earth in a resonant motion and dynamic action. Whereas consciousness in the inanimate matter is considered to remain dormant but active in the animate matter for the sake of convenience such differentiation has also been considered invalid, in view of the fact that all atoms are conscious of their own identity and existence. The so called 'Free Will' appears to be an acquired attribute of a self- assembled natural or artificially assembled **'machine system'** controlled by naturally inherent or artificial intelligence for survival and work under any given epigenetic environment. And scientists consider artificially intelligent gadgets to be also conscious entities. A big boulder lying in a field does not constitute a machine and just lies there as a lump of matter. The whole universe is therefore governed by the law of perpetual work in which; action and reaction, cause and effect and effort and destiny are all equal and opposite. This law of perpetual work is 'eternal', 'universal' and 'applicable' through all the time-scales, the past, the present and the future. Conscious or unconscious defiance, ignorance of this law or willfully contravening it, leads to certain destruction. Only adherence to this law, leads to a happy and harmonious survival, irrespective of cast, creed, color of the skin, religious faith at birth and physical location anywhere in the universe.

Work, nature of work and classification of work

Perhaps the first ever definition, description, characterization and classification of work has descended down to mankind from the 'Ved and Upanishads' the philosophical texts of India and then explained in relation to personal and social behavior and human psychology in the celestial song– 'The Bhagwad Geeta'. **Karma** (car-ma) is a word meaning the combined result of a person's actions as well as the actions itself and encapsulates in it's meaning the cycle of causes and their effects.[8-14] According to **the theory of Karma**, what happens to any person happens so, because they caused it with their actions.[8-14] The simple and succinct definition of work being- 'each and every physical action, deed or movement that is performed, consciously or unconsciously, willingly or unwillingly with cooperation of the mind, using all or any of the five senses, the various organs and limbs of our body, from morning to evening, during day and night, through weeks, months, years and all through the life, from the moment of birth to the last breath, is known as 'work' or Karma. And all the work performed have been classified into three categories, (i) **'Spontaneous work'**- work done on the spur of a moment or time which bears a reaction or result almost instantaneously, (ii) **'Cumulative work'**- work done that does not produce an immediate reaction and is kept in abeyance until an opportune time arrives for the delivery of its result. No corrective measures for such actions are either available or possible, (iii) **'Previously done or accumulated work'**- work done from the 'cumulative list' in another span of time that is ready to bear results. They are also commonly described by such synonyms as 'destiny', 'luck', 'fate' and 'fortune'. Just as human beings, animals, birds, fishes or microbial life forms have different gestation time frames until birth and every different crop plant species has its own crop growth period from the sowing of seeds to harvesting, so also each and every cumulative work done in life takes a definite time for producing their consequences or results. This time period from the moment, work is done, to the delivery of its result, may be over in just one life-span or may take several hundred cycles of birth and rebirth for an individual as it is generally believed *(here cycles of birth and rebirth only mean to suggest the number of times, the self-replicating DNA molecule is multiplied with its characteristic information coded on it before completely changing and erasing the memory of any particular experience or work. Otherwise, rebirth or re-incarnation of an individual after death is scientifically and technically impossible and continues to be a mis-interpreted popular myth perpetuated over ages).*[16,17] Rebirth or reincarnation is only possible as regeneration of the characteristic traits and attributes in a new individual born, by the routine self-replicating process of the DNA in association with its epigenetic environment and certainly not as a rebirth of an individual, once he is dead. It is in fact a **'*Gunarjanma*'** which is a repeated regeneration of characteristic quality traits (Guna) arising out of the cyclic self-replication of DNA under a changing epigenetic environment and not the repeated rebirth **'*Punarjanma*'** *(Janma as in birth)* of any individual after his or her death.[16-18] How, where, and in what form, the information and memory about the work done or experiences in life are recorded, stored and carried to the next birth and their consequences then encoded for execution in the new form of program loaded in the human genome-DNA, is an unresolved mystery. However, recent developments in the field of molecular genetics are gradually resolving these issues. What seems almost certain is that the human brain cannot be the vehicle or a carrier of this memory from one life to the other, although, brain is used as a tool to control and coordinate all activities in a body during life time in all animals? The phenomena appears to be working at the level of the arrangement and rearrangement of the base-pairs (Adenine, Cytosine, Thymine and Guanine) sequencing of the DNA molecules or at the sub-quantum level of an intense subtle energy or energy field, about which nothing or very little scientific knowledge is known as yet. Changes in the sequence of Base Pairs on DNA would mean a drastic change (mutation) of species itself and this appears to be impossible. However, recording of the memory of experiences suffered by any uni- or multi-cellular organism may be possible during the process of self-replication of the DNA molecules and their methylation. DNA- methylation is an epigenetic mechanism used by living cells to control their gene expression. A number of other mechanisms also exist to control gene expression in eukaryotes, but DNA-methylation is a commonly used epigenetic signaling tool that can fix genes in the "off" position.

Methylation is a critical process that happens trillions of times in the life time of every living cell. It is one of the most essential metabolic functions of the body and is responsible for the synthesis of a variety of enzymes and proteins, within individual cells, as a result of the stimulus received by the cell membrane from the epigenetic environment around it. Dynamically, adapting to stress and the challenges of life, arising from the sudden or gradual changes in epigenetic environment, as a strategy for survival is the essential aspect of the DNA-methylation process. Scientists have also discovered how vital the DNA-methylation is to a number of other cellular processes such as embryonic development, X-chromosome inactivation, genomic imprinting, gene suppression, carcinogenesis and chromosome stability and links of aberrations in methylation patterns to several human diseases with significant correlations. These findings could be important in aiding the development of appropriate therapies and for understanding and preventing conditions that develop right from the beginning of zygotic and embryonic development as a result of abnormal methylation of the X chromosome *(inherited either from the father or the mother)* and gene imprinting.[19,20] DNA-Methylation does not change the existing sequence of base pairs in the DNA molecule but modifies the configuration by masking some parts of the base-pair sequences on DNA and thereby reading the coded information differently to synthesize new enzymes and proteins in accordance with this masking, during self-replication. DNA-methylation is the process through which a methyl group (- CH_3) is added to DNA nucleotides, very often to the fifth carbon atom of a cytosine ring. This conversion of cytosine bases to 5- methylcytosine is catalyzed by DNA methyltransferases (DNMTs). These modified cytosine residues usually lay next to a (G) guanine base (CpG methylation) and the result is two methylated cytosines positioned diagonally to each other on opposite strands of the DNA double helix. DNA-methylation occurs at CpG sites—i.e. the sites where a cytosine (C) is immediately in front of a guanine (G). When a CpG segment in the promoter region of a gene is methylated, the expression of the gene is suppressed (i.e. it is turned off). The extent of addition of methyl groups is controlled at several levels in cells and is carried out by a family of enzymes called DNA methyltransferases (DNMTs). Defects in DNA-methylation can result in disorders affecting embryogenesis, genomic imprinting and even the onset of cancer. The other important purpose of DNA-methylation is the formation of the chromatin structure, which enables a single cell (also called a stem cell) to grow into a complex multi-cellular organism made up of different tissues and organs.[19-22]

The new science of epigenetics

The science of *epigenetics* has been an associated component of the entire evolutionary process of biological life on the Earth. However, its role as an independent subject of study was established barely one and quarter century ago, almost simultaneously when the theoretical geneticists were busy in creating a dogmatic belief system that all life forms are the products of their destiny, encoded in their Genes (DNA). The immaculately crucial experiments, conducted on somatic and enucleated cells over a century ago, laid the foundation of the modern science of *epigenetics* which essentially means "control above and beyond genetics'. Three decades of research in *epigenetics* has almost established that the inherited DNA encoded blueprints at the time of birth by any life form, is certainly not its destiny! Environmental conditions such as; nutrition, physical, physiological, psychological state of the mother during intra-uterine gestation period, influence and modify inherited genes without changing their basic blueprint. And the so called 'Environment' includes grossly measurable terrestrial and atmospheric parameters, besides the subtle and almost immeasurable, cosmic and universal influences. However, in the enthusiasm of in depth studies of the DNA, the equally crucial role of chromosomal proteins in heredity was inadvertently neglected. The science of *epigenetics* is re-establishing the importance of those chromosomal proteins. [19-22]

In the chromosome, the DNA *(deoxyribonucleic acid)* forms the core, and the proteins cover this core like a sleeve. When the genes are covered, their information cannot be 'read'. In order to remove the cover off, an environmental signal is needed to spur the sleeve proteins to change their shape and get detached from the core-DNA double helix, and thereby permitting the gene to be read. Once the DNA is uncovered, the cell makes a copy of the exposed gene. The activity of the gene is thereby controlled by the presence or absence of the proteins that en-sleeved it, which in turn are controlled and regulated by the external environment. The science of '*epigenetics*' explains how environmental signals control the activity of the genes. The hitherto understood 'Primacy of the Genes' has now been revised to the 'Primacy of the Environment' and the new scheme of flow of information in cell biology, first begins with an environmental signal, passing over to the regulatory protein and only then to the *Deoxyribonucleic acid* (DNA) and *Ribonucleic acid* (RNA) and to the end product, which is also a protein. Therefore, both the two mechanisms 'genes' and 'environment' contribute equally to determining the behavior of humans and all other life forms. Thousands of variations of synthesized proteins can be produced from the same gene blueprint on DNA by environmentally controlling the regulatory proteins. And such environmentally influenced finely-tuned gene can get passed on to generation after generation. Today, the genes are now believed to be far more fluid and responsive to even minutest changes in the environment. Neither the Genes nor the cell nucleus, where they reside are now considered as the proverbial brain of the cell and control its biology. Biological cells are indeed shaped and regulated by the epigenetic environment in which they live and survive.[19-22]

The mechanism of DNA-methylation

A series of experiments have established that 'methyl chemical group (-CH3)' is essentially involved in epigenetic modification of information encoded on the gene. When the methyl groups get attached to the DNA of a gene, they change the way the regulatory chromosomal proteins are bound to the DNA molecule. When they are bound too tight to the gene, the protein sleeve cannot be removed from over the gene to be read for transcription and multiplication. The perpetually continuous and dynamic process of 'DNA-methylation' is therefore the most essential component of any biological cell mechanism as its strategy for survival in a given environmental condition. There is convincing evidence that programming of health for entire life time of a child to be born are as much affected by the intra uterine conditions in the womb of the mother as the genes in determining our mental attitude to physical performance in life. Any modification is easy to understand when it is incorporated on the DNA itself (mutation). However, the most commonly observed modification on DNA happens when a C base is followed by a G base. This sequence is designated as CpG, and constitutes the site where enzymes secreted within cells are able to add a methyl (CH_3) group to the cystosine base. In case, a large number of CpG motifs are present in any section of DNA, a large number of methyl groups can be added epigenetically. This attracts specific proteins to the sites to repress expression of those genes. DNA methylation carried on a large number of CpG motifs lying in close proximity to each other produces exceptional effects. With methylation, the DNA changes its shape and the gene is completely switched off. And the gene remains switched off not just in that cell but in all the daughter cells that are multiplied when it divides. In case of the non-dividing cells such as the neuron cells of the brain, the patterns of DNA methylation are possibly established while a child is still in the womb of his/her mother and that pattern practically remains in place throughout the life of that child to be born. Mechanism of permanently switching genes off, during the life time of an individual through DNA methylation has provided scientists to study the root causes for the drastic variations in characteristics, behavior, attitudes, physiology, psychology and intellectual capabilities between identical paternal and monozygotic twins. Identical paternal and monozygotic twins begin to diverge epigenetically during individual development in the uterus and differ in their DNA methylation patterns. The differences between monozygotic twins become more pronounced with advancing age and exposure to different environments.

All the 30-70 trillion individual cells constituting a human body, irrespective of their function as cells of sweat gland, skin, muscle, eyelids, bone cartilage or neurons in the brain, essentially contain the same genetic code, the DNA. These specialized cells only use the information present in those genes in different ways, depending on their functional requirements. For example, in brain neuron cells, the genes responsible for producing haemoglobin are heavily methylated and they remain permanently switched off throughout life. However, in the cells that produce red blood cells, these genes are not methylated and they continue to produce haemoglobin, throughout life. Fortunately, DNA-methylation is a pretty stable configuration to keep certain genes permanently switched off. However, when our cells have to respond to short-term changes encountered in environment, they switch on to a second type of mechanism, called the 'histone protein adjustment to genes' to modulate the expression of a gene. In view of a large number of amino acids that can be modified on histone proteins and the fact that more than 60 different chemical groups can be loaded on amino acids, thousands of combinations of 'histone modifications' on the same or different genes in different cell types can be made possible. And all cells interpret these histone modifications in a different way. In a very simple language, Nessa Carrey has defined DNA-methylation as akin to the on/off switch and histone modification as the volume control.[19, 20]

Epigenetic mechanisms have also been identified to be an important factor in a variety of diseases besides cancer and cardiovascular disease and diabetes. Only 5-6% of cardiovascular and cancer patients attribute their disease to heredity, whereas ninety five percent of the breast and other cancers have been observed to be derived from the environmentally induced epigenetic alterations and certainly not because of the defective genes. Drastic changes in diet, nutrition and lifestyles of prostate cancer patients for three months or more have been found to be sufficient to switch off the activity of over 500 genes, which were responsible for the formation of their tumors. No wonder, it is here, we realize the cardinal importance of the Vedic Indian philosophical wisdom, when it calls upon human beings to be particular about their diet, nutrition and breathing.

Epigenetics in Relation to the Inherited and Accumulated Work (Karma) *Epigenetics* is a rapidly developing area of human genetics and has assumed practically the same importance as the project on sequencing of the Human Genome. Science of *epigenetics*, has accelerated research into inherited (***Prarabdha-Karma)*** diseases and cancer and it is anticipated that initiatives to evolve a standard definition of the 'normal human *epigenome' (if that should ever be possible?)* will further enhance progress towards better understanding of the role of *epigenetics* in human diseases. The sequential program of base pairs on the DNA of the sperm from the father at the time of its fertilization in the egg cell of the mother is the inherited work or the so called the '***Prarabdh Karma***' of the child to be born. Since no one can choose his or her parents for birth, there is no option but to accept the '***Prarabdh Karma***' as a continuing link with the ancestors. Unfortunately, James Watson and Francis Crick in 1953, while announcing the discovery of the double helix structure of the DNA molecule, created, a somewhat dogmatic belief system that every living organism is a product of his/her destiny and is likely to suffer as per the program encoded on the inherited DNA. Whereas, this may be partially true, the inherited DNA also gets continuously modified according to experience gained by the new-to be- born individual, right from its zygotic state, in surviving against the changing intra-uterine epigenetic environment, and continuing to do so after birth, growth, maturity to death. The survival strategy, during life cycle, is faithfully recorded on its DNA by means of the perpetual methylation process and is called the accumulated work or the '***Sanchit Karma***'. Epigenetics involves, chemical changes to DNA that prevent or enhance the reading of a base pair sequence. The precise mechanism involves, the addition of methyl groups to a gene and thereby modify, its transcription for a specific metabolic action. Early experiences recorded on our DNA not only shape our mind but they literally change how our body metabolism and physiology work at a fundamental level. Recent researches[19-21] suggest, a very strong association of significant decline in health in adulthood for a wide variety of socio-economic reasons and particularly due to poverty and mal-nutrition during childhood. And according to Professor Candace B. Pert,[23] it is the nature and amount of proteins, enzymes and hormones synthesized within the body systems that are vital for breathing, feeding, getting rid of waste, reproducing and all the other activities that characterize the living organisms. These proteins, enzymes, hormones generate and control our thoughts, induce actions and change behavior as our dynamic response to the minutest variations in epigenetic environment. The signatures of epigenetic changes have the potential to be carried on to several generations of self- replications of DNA in its inheritance. The story of the revolution in epigenetic science has been beautifully discussed and documented by Nessa Carey in her two books.[19, 20] Still however, approach to the subject from neurological science suggests a strong association and correlation between ultra- structural differences in the gross neuron-anatomical features of cortical symmetries or asymmetries in human brains with the display of exceptional abilities of talented individuals.

Pure and impure work

All the three categories of work have further been divided into two types; **'Pure work'** and **'Impure work'**, suggesting to mean that any work which is done, strictly in accordance with the laws of nature, is 'pure work' and that which is accomplished, either willfully or accidentally, without strictly adhering to the science involved behind the work, is called the 'impure work'. Today, if giant aero planes, with hundreds of human passengers or several tons of cargo, on- board are successfully flying across continents and oceans, is not because man has conquered nature but only because we are flying them strictly by adhering to and in accordance with the laws of nature, discovered by science and enable us, to do so. This is the reason, why scientists (physicists in particular) as a general rule crave, desire and work for uniform universal standards of measures for all physical quantities and for quality of materials. Further, the entire universe is well known to be rhythmic, cyclic and perfectly periodic in nature. And in keeping with this periodicity of the universe in general, cyclic nature of birth and rebirth *(as is believed for thousands of years)* is no more left to be a speculation or a fiction of blind religious faith but a scientifically established truth, governed in accordance with the 'law of work'. The only change being, that, rebirth or reincarnation taking place is not that of any individual from the historical past but it is a routine process of perpetual self-replication of the DNA molecules and near identical replication and regeneration of characteristic traits, reflected into new individuals born which includes all the uni- and multi-cellular animate life forms in nature, including plants. The DNA molecule is now believed to be constantly evolving itself by incorporating the experience gained during its interaction for survival under changing epigenetic environmental conditions by suitably changing the configuration of the sequences of base-pairs into its DNA structure and synthesis of suitable proteins as a strategy for survival of the organism. Therefore, scientifically and technically, the ancient concept of 'rebirth or reincarnation' of any individual is just impossible and continues to be a popular myth since thousands of years. The probability of near-exact replication of specific characteristics and personal traits, exhibited by an individual from the historical past, into a new born individual, at random is the only possibility left to explain our understanding about rebirth. And repeated replication and generation of specific traits under interaction with specific epigenetic environmental conditions is a routine characteristic property of the self-replicating DNA molecules. Unfortunately, such random coincidence of resemblance of characteristic traits with someone from the historical past is generally understood to be the cases of rebirth or reincarnation.[16-18] Even otherwise, for the sake of our belief in 'rebirth or reincarnation', we only compare similarities of characteristic traits, thoughts, behavior and actions and not the physical body structures, appearance or features. I am aware that under the dogmatic influence of meta-narrative books for hundreds of generations, it is not easy for any individual to dare so easily and change his / her opinion or even be receptive to a contrarian view point. This is because, practically everyone has been made to believe in the idea of rebirth by someone most revered or dear to them since their childhood. A very good compilation of comparative similarities of characteristic musical artistic excellence and traits, amongst a large number of cases of individuals, born between a wide interval of time, in India and abroad, as cases of 'plausible rebirths' has been published by Vidyadhar Gopal Oke[18]. What is satisfying to the author of this article being, that Vidyadhar Gopal Oke, has very correctly coined the term –*'Gunarjanma'*– meaning rebirth of characteristic qualities and traits (Guna) in lieu of the ancient term- *'Reincarnation or Rebirth or Punarjanma'* which has been grossly misinterpreted or misunderstood for thousands of years.[16,17]

The process of accumulating work, the 'sanchit (accumulated) karma', the concept of mythological character 'chitragupta' who writes down the details of our good and bad karma done from birth to death and human obligations. The natural process of incorporating experiences gained by an organism on its DNA molecule, as a part of its strategy for survival in a changing epigenetic environment, by rearranging sequences of Adenosine, Thymine, Guanine and Cytosine base-pair molecules (A, T, G, C) by way of natural or artificially induced mutation, or masking certain sections of their sequence during self- replication through 'DNA-methylation' is a *de-facto* process involved in, recording experience gained by a individual cells of an organism, in dynamically adjusting internal physiology to the changing epigenetic environment outside, for their survival. This recording, of the work done, during struggle for survival is what is known as the 'accumulated work' OR the 'Sanchit Karma'. Most logically, the perpetually dynamic process of 'DNA-mythylation' going on in every individual cell of a living organism by recording the changes in its epigenetic environment and corresponding synthesis of essential enzymes, hormones and proteins as a strategy for survival,[19-21] may in fact be corresponding to the concept of **'Chitragupta', (Figure 3)**[22] the Indian mythological Assistant of 'Yamaraj' the Deity of death. 'Chitragupta', as an integral functionary of the Deity of Death, has been assigned the task of keeping an in-depth track record of all the good and bad work (good or aberrant mutations or methylations) done by the living organisms, from their birth to death and help Yamaraj in deciding the fate of all that work for the future. According to a fascinating and perhaps prophetic legend in India, 'Chitragupt', was secretly (Gupt) conceived and mentally pictured (Chitra) by the creator of the Universe – 'Bramha' in its mind as a humanlike figure holding a paper and an ink-pot in his hands with a sword girdled to his waist. He was therefore named as 'Chitragupta' and empowered to dispense justice and punish those who violated the 'Dharma', which means the natural scientific laws for survival in doing their work and not any religion or religious belief. Curiously enough and quite logically, the ink-pen in the hand of Chitragupta suggests to the record of dynamically changing epigenetic environment around the organism that triggers rewriting, modification or masking of the genetic information on the DNA molecules, and onset of metabolic sequential events within cells in consequence.

Figure 3. Symbolic Idol of 'Chitragupta' holding a pen made of peacock feather and an ink pot in his left hand. As Assistant of Lord Yama the deity of death, Chitragupta has the mandate to keep writing the details of Karma using his pen till there is ink in the inkpot and thereafter use his sword to strike death. *(Reproduced from Home/devotional/Chitragupta Maharaj (Lord Chitragupta) Best and Beautiful hd wallpapers/photos free down load, April 17, 2019 from the web)*[22]

And obviously, the symbolic 'paper' in the hands of 'Chitragupta' is this writing of the record of the 'work' through the 'DNA-methylation' process. Once methylation is completed, the organism undergoes its life according to the new sequential program encoded on the DNA. **Therefore, work, its nature, cause and effects have a continuing link to the genetic make-up of the DNA molecules.**[20,21] And specific characteristic traits, qualities, physique, physiology and psychology of the new individual born would be the reflection of new set of proteins synthesized in accordance with the modified sequence of its DNA. Such changes, though incredibly small have profound implications on the overall personality of any individual. What is certain being that every work done *(considered here only in respect of human beings for obvious reasons)* will have its reaction, every cause will have its effect and every effort done has its destiny within a time frame which is specific to the kind and nature of the work done. **It is in keeping with this truth, that every human being is born with individual specific characteristic traits, potential, capacity and ability for specific kind and nature of his 'delineated work'.**[16-21] Not only this, but nature has also provided to every individual born as a human being, an opportunity to wipe out or correct the results of the cumulative work encoded on his DNA through his/her focused conscious efforts in rearranging the sequenced program. And this is achievable with conscious regular practice of controlling breath, mind and thoughts. Our, success, personal satisfaction and salvation lie only in identifying and recognizing our 'nature-delineated' work, understanding the responsibilities involved in doing our delineated work and performing that to the best of our potential, capacity and ability. This is indeed the secret of all those successful people in any society, anywhere in the world. Complexities arise because of incorrect recognition and the choices made in choosing the nature and kind of delineated work under incorrect guidance, emotion, coercion, compulsion, intimidation, threat, perceived greed for monetary gain and desire or for any such reasons. Whereas, the compromise so made under any such circumstances might successfully provide education, employment and sufficient livelihood to an individual for life but not the inherent satisfaction of personal accomplishment. No wonder, innumerable individuals can be found in any society all over the world, willingly pursuing entirely different work than what they were educated and trained for. **What seems to be marvelous is, how the 'Rishis' from the Vedic Period in India could have conceived, understood and personified the concept and functions of 'Chitragupta' which is akin to the function of the process of 'DNA-methylation' discovered by** the modern science of molecular genetics and its fundamental role in the life of any living organism.[22]

The truth in this fact can be best realized through individual introspection and personal experiences rather than through a debate. Personal experiences very often become the determinant of the personal convictions in regard to the performance of the delineated work. Unfortunately, academic universities in most countries, instead of restricting their role in moulding philosophers and thinkers and engaging primarily in creating new knowledge, are taking upon themselves, the role of running training schools for job and employment- oriented professional trades for commercial reasons. This activity should have best been left exclusively to the polytechnics or technical schools meant for the purpose.

Natural delineation of work, their signals and responsibility of parents

The implications of work, therefore, are not only linked to the very creation of the universe but extend to everything that forms a part of the universe. The entire universe is governed by the 'Law of Karma', which is absolutely impersonal, incorruptible, beyond manipulation and free from any intervention. There is therefore no option before human beings but to submit and accept what is offered to them by the nature. And this offer comes to human beings as signal- indications in the form of inherent abilities such as; natural aptitude, inclination for certain kinds of work, inner urge, compulsive self motivation, convictions, dedication, determination, independent thinking and inherent will to perform, sharp memory, alertness, keen observation, ability to quickly grasp specific knowledge, open and receptive mind and will to change without bias or prejudice. These attributes provide the necessary guide to seek, accept and complete the delineated work. Successful parenthood therefore lies in recognizing such indications in their children and in providing all necessary help to them in making the correct choice.

Interdependence for work in societies and division of labour

The fundamental periodic re-cycling characteristic of nature is clearly evident from the fact that one kind of life-form is a food for the survival of the other kind of life as a part of the food-chain. What is excreted by one life-form as waste becomes the food for survival of the other.

In this process, what each form of life is factually doing being; it is picking up the atoms and molecules of the basic food-elements which are essentially required to maintain the biochemical, physiological and physical functions of its own body for healthy existence as an individual. And since the elements so essentially required for our existence are cosmic in origin, all life forms are indirectly linked to the cosmic universe.

Like the component interdependence in a food chain, human society is also interdependent on a number of individuals who carry out many types of physical, intellectual and social work for its requirement as a group, community or a nation. In this spirit of interdependence, upholding the dignity of labor, it is totally wrong to claim or maintain superiority or inferiority of one kind of job over the other. All kinds of jobs are complementary and equally important. It is the disproportionate monetary pay structures devised by the humans or unavoidable dirtying hands in doing some kind of jobs that have created such social divide. However, irrespective of any country, community, society and civilization in the history and at present, allotment of work to individuals has actually been based on mental, intellectual and physical capacity of each individual. In the absence of regular training schools in large numbers in the historical past, useful practical trades were handed down from the forefathers and parents to the children through generations. Carrying forward this tradition of work with conviction and motivation by children used to become means of his inward advancement, improvement, improvisation, innovation, research and development. No wonder all this lead to the establishment of family trades and professions. Such families pursuing different trades without rivalry or jealousy complemented each other and helped in maintaining a harmonious society at large. Today, with development of science and technology, the number of new practical trades and professions for livelihood has multiplied thousand fold. It is practically impossible to expect people to stick to the traditional family-trades under the changed scenario. Despite these developments and changes, the fundamental natural 'Law of Work' stays inviolate. People in all societies, communities and countries, consciously or unconsciously, continue to still get classified / segregated into four type of job categories, namely; (i) those that are creating new knowledge (ii) those that help in protecting the society interests (iii) those who venture into trading and transport of essential commodities for the society and (iv) those, who help in maintaining cleanliness, community hygiene and environmental aesthetics. Today, the number of various kinds of jobs falling within each of the above category has increased with technological and industrial progress. However, such classification actually evolves and comes out more from the inherent inclination, temperament, aptitude or compulsions arising out of the actions on the part of the individual himself, strictly in accordance with the 'Law of Work' than merely from inheritance and birth. Every individual is responsible himself for the kind of job that comes to his fold and nobody else can be held responsible. Fortunately, under the current economic scenario, each one of us is expected to routinely perform all the four types of jobs for himself / herself, if not for others.

Ethical and moral obligations in performance of work

Having been pushed into doing our delineated work, it becomes our duty to carry out the same with utmost capacity, ability and sincerity. Any negligence in doing that work gets reflected in consequences that befall on the society besides disrupting the entire chain of interdependent community life. Therefore, creating sensitivity, sensibility and preparing mind-set in moulding young generation since childhood for a disciplined and duty-bound community life, becomes the primary responsibility of parents at home and teachers in schools and should form the first lessons of the beginning of a formal education. The level of discipline becomes more and more rigorous with progress in education and higher responsibilities of work. And surely, this is impossible to handle and carry forward without adhering to the 'laws of nature' and the 'law of work'. Craving and working for reward and recognition for doing the 'delineated work', tantamount to bargain and is a sign of an individual with a weak mind, lacking self-esteem and respect. At the same time a judicious, responsible and responsive authority is ever expected to identify, recognize and encourage good worker and good piece of work done. Conflicts arise when exploitation for gain and profit overrides all other considerations due to systemic deficiencies, subversions, sabotage or collective failure on the part of community to check such malaise.

Dictionaries describe 'ethics' as a science of moral principles or moral duty and 'morality' as concerned with right or wrong conduct in practicing virtue. Ethical and moral conduct in human behaviour, though complex, is certainly not exclusive to him / her because all forms of living creatures exhibit practicing their ethical and moral responsibilities in raising, rearing, feeding and protecting their progenies to their best of capacity until the progenies are on their own. And such other responsibilities as keeping vigil and protection against natural predators, hunting in groups and sharing food etc. are carried out by them both individually and collectively in groups or herds. The performance of work on ethical basis is not comparable to 'duty-bound' work done. The concept of 'ethics' lays more in human imagination and cannot possibly be generalized as being common in all living organisms.

Obligations, responsibilities and conduct for scientists

Scientists from all disciplines, all nationalities and communities have been individually and collectively responsible for the material progress made and comforts provided to human kinds. They not only create new knowledge but transform that into useful products for mass production, consumption, use and comfort thereby containing or at least restraining jealousies, rivalries amongst populace who have and have-not. However, it is the sagacity and responsibility of the knowledgeable, sagacious, enlightened and the ruling class of human beings to exploit new knowledge for the benefit and welfare of masses and curb the destructive / harmful use of the same. **Almost all scientists pursue science essentially to satisfy their intellectual curiosity.** They propose hypothesis without parochialism, blind-beliefs and work hard to seek evidence for or against the hypothesis. A meager piece of new information discovered can be a starting point for a new industry and provides enough excitement and inspiration to them to continue their pursuit. In the olden days, scientists in general used to avoid or hide curiosity in public, about investigations in the fields such as; spirituality, mind, the aura fields, morphic and morphogenetic fields, paranormal, psychokinetic, consciousness, out of body experiences or even life after death phenomena for they were considered to be out of scientific culture for investigation. However, the rise and growth of 'Quantum Physics', 'Theory of Relativity', elementary particle physics and cosmology and their implications in understanding the nature of reality, have demolished all barriers, inhibitions, skepticism, reservations, prejudices, biases and dogmas in the study of these or related phenomena as problems of scientific inquiry. **A true-scientist is therefore expected to be open**

to every kind of possibility and approaches to solving a particular problem in a multi-disciplinary effort. He should not be averse to considering every possible idea, how so ever bizarre it might appear, just because there is no precedent investigation reported on this line of approach. Today, any kind of scientific enquiry, starting from any discipline converges at the end on the ultimate nature of realty, the consciousness and its manifestation. Therefore, scientists are best advised to remain aware of the spectacular revolutionary developments in physics besides confining themselves to their own branch of science. After all physics and its laws form the under-current of all scientific investigations. Who knows, carrying new ideas from seemingly unrelated discipline to your own may provide new understanding in your field of investigation? What is important being to keep the flame of inner urge and passion for new knowledge constantly burning within the heart, without fear, bias, prejudice and pride? One of the most successful public educators Mr. Shiv Khera maintains- "Winners don't do different things, they do things differently". Lord Krishna in the 'Srimad Bhagwad Geeta' also pronounces ***"Yogah Karmasu Koushalam",*** meaning "Any work accomplished to perfection with utmost sincerity and to the best of one's ability is Yoga".

References for further reading:

1. Rousseau Pierre., 'From Atom to Star', S Chand & Co. 1987, pp78.

2. Emsley, John., 'Nature's Building Blocks- An A-Z Guide to the Elements, Oxford University Press, 2001, pp539.

3. Hey, Tony and Walters Patrick., 'The New Quantum Universe' Cambridge University Press, 2004, pp357.

4. Rees Martin., 'Just Six Numbers', Phoenix (1999).

5. Weinberg, Steven., 'The Discovery of Subatomic Particles, Cambridge University Press (2003).

6. Stenger, Victor J., 'The Comprehensible Cosmos: Where Do the Laws of Physics Come From?, Prometheus Books (2006).

7. Weinberg, Steven., 'The First Three Minutes : A Modern View of the Origin of the Universe' Basic Books (1993).

8. Guney, M. R., 'Dynaneshwari chey Bhava Vishwa' in Marathi, Snehal Prakashan, Pune, 2006, pp192.

9. Guney, M. R., 'Geetartha Vishwa' in Marathi (annotated with Commentary and translation in English by the author himself), Snehal Prakashan, Pune, 2005, pp 297.

10. Athaley, Keshav Ganesh., Critical Commentary on Shri Dasbodh by Samartha Swami Ramdas, 'Shri Dasbodh-Gudhartha Deepika' in Marathi, Shri Dasbodh Gudhartha Deepika Prakashan Mandal, Indore & Ujjain, India, 1993, pp.710.

11. Vivekananda, Swami., 'Karma Yog' Ramakrishna Mission

12. Pujyashri Chandrasekharendra Sarasvatisvamigal., Shankaracharya of Kanchi Kamakoti Peetha., 'Hindu-Dharma-The Universal Way of Life- Voice of the Guru', Bharatiya Vidya Bhavan, Bombay, 1995, pp 790.

13. 'Eight Upanishads', Vol.1 (Isa, Kena, Katha and Taittiriya), Translated by Swami Gambhiranand., Advaita Ashram, Calcutta, 1972, pp 408.

14. Thakkar, Hirabhai., 'Theory of Karma' English Translation of original in Gujrati, Kusum Prakashan, Ahmedabad, India, 2001,pp 80.

15. Sheldrake, Rupert., 'The Hypothesis of A New Science of Life- Morphic Resonance', Park Street Press, 1995, pp 272.

16. Moharir, Anil Vishnu., 'A Scientific Look at the Concept of Soul: An Attempted Synthesis', Zorba Books, Gurugram, 2017. And

17. Moharir, Anil Vishnu., 'Questions about Soul and Rebirth: Need for a Fresh Look and Re-definition', Paper Presented at the National Conference on Ancient Science and Technology, Retrospection and Aspirations (ASTRA-2015) Fergusson College, University of Pune, January 10-11, 2015. Proceedings of the Conference, ISSN. 2321-7715. Reg. No. 67495 / 97. Academy of Sanskrit Research. Melkote-571 431.

18. Oke, Vidyadhar Gopal., 'Punarjanma : Mithya ki Tatthya' in Marathi (Reincarnation : Myth or Truth', Param Mitra Publications, Thane, Maharashtra, India, 2018, pp 259.

19. Nessa Carey., 'The Epigenetic Revolution : How Modern Biology is Rewriting our Understanding of Genetics, Disease and Inheritance' Icon Books Ltd, 2012, pp 339.

20. Nessa Carey., 'Junk DNA : A Journey Through the Dark Matter of the Genome' Icon Books Ltd, 2015, pp340.

21. Lipton, Bruce H., 'Biology of Belief : Unleashing the Power of Consciousness, Matter & Miracles', Hay House, 2008.

22. Home/devotional/Chitragupta Maharaj (Lord Chitragupta) Best and Beautiful hd wallpapers/photos free down load, April 17, 2019 from the web).

23. Pert, Candace B., Molecules of Emotion: Why You Feel the Way You Feel, Pocket Books, 1997.

Acknowledgement

The author acknowledges with gratitude the help given by Prof. Dr. Ravin L. Thatte, M.S. FRCS (Edin.), Mumbai; Dr. T. P. Rajendran, Ex- Asstt. Director General, ICAR; and Prof. Dr. S. R. Bhat, LBS Centre for Plant Biotechnology, IARI, New Delhi; for reviewing the draft copy of this article, encouragement and suggesting useful editorial changes.

CHAPTER – 11

Towards Excellence in Science: Indian Perspective*

Introduction and brief historical

Man is born for knowledge and human mind is unique for its inquisitiveness. This trait unlike in other animals does not end with observation of an event but in making practical use of it and in coming to a logical conclusion. Thus, science grows as a search for 'truth' on the basis of the events taking place in the vicinity and around an individual and as Jacob Bronowski (1908-1974) the British Mathematician and Biologist describes– "science is our greatest spiritual adventure". However, it must be conceded that other organisms be it cattle or birds, also attempt a search for truth in their own way and use it for their individual or collective benefit. It is for nothing that we see a herd of cows heading towards home at dusk on their own and birds flying long distances at the dawn, returning to their roost, using their unique navigational abilities. We do not know or know very little of how they have developed their science and how they use it in their own society? The human intellect, however, despite his most developed brain, can still get confused between excellence and mediocrity. At times, we are made to believe that Albert Einstein, Gregore Mendel, Charles Darwin and many others, primarily engaged themselves in trying to intentionally seek excellence in science. But the truth is that the excellence they achieved was in fact a direct consequence of their self-motivation, inner urge and insatiable hunger for seeking new knowledge. Superlatives are often attached to their work only after they have achieved something credible. They did not tread the beaten path. Srinivasa Ramanujam, Jagadish Chandra Bose, Meghnad N. Saha, Sir Chandrasekhar Venkata Raman and many others actually worked hard to satisfy their incessant curiosity, and excellence they acquired was a mere fall out as a result of that. They volunteered to be prepared for personal sacrifices. C. V. Raman resigned his lucrative job in the Indian Revenue Services during the British rule for the sake of his convictions to pursue research in physics. Yes, some of them were indeed fiercely competitive in their ideas and observations to make new discoveries because of their superior intellect, keenest observations, analytical reasoning, sincerity of purpose and unshakable confidence in their personal ability. They did not feel it necessary to be crazy to influence any one in authority for recognition, excellence or for reward. Competition is an unavoidable and even essential aspect of human nature in any effort involving numerous people from numerous places, attempting to solve a common problem. And such competition in any enterprise can at times take very ugly forms. There have indeed been cases of occasional cheating, falsification of experimental observations and such others, but these get certainly rectified in the universal scientific referral system, where checking and crosschecking of claims is mandatory. There is no hierarchy in scientific research and certainly no linkage to advanced age and doing good science. In fact, most of the Nobel laureates accomplished their feats between 25 to 35 years of their age. It is here; the spiritual aspect and dimensions of all we have learnt counts and matters. Whereas, all attempts must be maintained to sustain a healthy competition, we must do everything at our command to diminish its nastier manifestations. A practical example of nastier aspect of introducing excessive competition at all levels of education has culminated in recording the highest juvenile crimes in Japan at one time after the end of the second World War, when each student wanted to eliminate his immediate competitor.

History of science is a witness to the fact that at times, search for truth or 'science' because of rational thinking of the pioneer minds came in conflict with the blind religious faith adhered to by the Church authorities of those times in Europe. Such conflicts in the Indian continents have never been heard off ever since the Vedic times but there are elaborate descriptions of great scholarly debates, contesting some specific interpretations of the Vedic Texts. Contrary to the scenario witnessed in Europe, India and the Indian people have always welcomed new thinking, new concepts, philosophy and even religions from every place on the earth. This is the reason, why practically every religious philosophy known, exists in India with sizeable adherents. Prevalent thinking on religion and philosophy in Europe were both the prerogative and privilege of those so-called sagacious individuals, patronized by the local kings and monarchs, who always tried to dominate and influence the rulers. Slightest departure from their ideas without consent or approval, invited inevitable wrath, condemnation, deportation or even death on charges of misleading or misguiding the youth of those times. Despite these difficulties, science and scientists continued to receive patronage and freedom to express views at times from some very progressive, sagacious, broad and open-minded Monarchs and Kings. Those pursuing science were generally considered very learned and endowed with better intellectual faculties. They occupied eminent positions as advisors in royal courts, as teachers in universities and learned societies to impart knowledge to others. Persons such as Socrates or Aristotle fell in this category. However, situations arose when scientific findings and their experimental confirmation came in direct conflict with interests of the Religious Church authorities.

Hence, Plato was accused of corrupting young minds and was forced to drink poison by the dogmatic church authorities that were incapable of appreciating his radical ideas, leave aside comprehending. Several other original scientific thinkers were also persecuted and made to suffer for their holding views different from those of the church. For centuries, the Church stood in shame and ridicule for perpetrating injustice for these events and only towards the close of the twentieth century the Pope publicly begged pardon and ordered re-trial of all those sacrificed scientists, philosophers and thinkers who suffered at the hands of the church authorities in the past and pronounce them 'Not-Guilty'.

Therefore, the inherent urge for seeking truth with sound logic and reasoning which initially attracted only the innovative, adventurous intellectuals also started attracting and influencing the knowledgeable, open-minded and supportive politicians and thereby the makers of state policies. Initially, even Charles Darwin and Gregor Mendel also did not get major support or appreciation from the state. Recognition and support from the State for excellence in science therefore became important and pre-requisite for search for truth, propagation of scientific facts, education and for economic benefit of the subjects at large. Because, no responsible government in any form can allow spread of falsehood, ignorance, rebellion or unrest amongst masses in any form. Once the excellence in science or innovative ideas started getting support and patronage from the rulers and politicians, it became essential for scientists to clamour around the ruling class to garner support for funding and early priority for execution of their projects on grounds of economic urgency to better quality of governance, or lifestyle of the masses. The conduct and practice of Science no longer remained a mere intellectual exercise but evolved as a major instrument of change for any responsible and responsive government in any part of the world. Quality of scientific and political leadership assumed importance not only for the generation of wealth for a nation but in providing economic, livelihood, employment and food security for the deprived. No wonder, therefore, Science became an area of major vocational activity within both government and private sector and also as a joint venture between the two. The technological revolution in areas of nuclear, space, communication, transportation and several other sciences are the shining examples of the state supported scientific relationships and activities and their spin-off benefits. The multi-billion dollar Large Hadron Collider Project of the European Space Agency (CERN) is the most illuminating example of this kind.

As a fall-out of these developments, the competition for funding research projects became the major objective besides the search for truth, which got pushed into background. This is a glaring aberration for the activity, which was primarily considered pious, intellectual, peaceful, truthful, and spiritual, and for the benefit of the entire human community. A scientists' career advancement unfortunately was linked more not for doing good science and creating new knowledge but to the amount of funds mobilized by them and more for the magnitude of possible commercial exploitation of the society at large. It is just analogous to comparing spiritual poets like Kabir, Rahim, Surdas or Namdev with patronized poets / singers in the Royal courts, singing praise and kudos for charity. In the other words when "Science" is influencing industry, commerce and economics, the term excellence has assumed different meaning to different people, depending upon the intentions of the polity? Which face is the real excellence is difficult to comprehend. We have already reached the stage when we might say; beauty lies in the eyes of the beholder. However, as optimists we would still like to believe that real excellence could always be spotted, if we attempt it without impairing our judgment due to extraneous considerations of region or race. After all, excellence is not a monopoly of any cast, creed, community or that of a nation. It sprouts from the inner urge of an individual true to his conviction.

Accountability in science

Accountability is linked to excellence as it propels an individual or a group to work and produce results. Whether excellence is achieved or not is another matter. There are different levels of accountability such as individual, group, institutional, organizational and on the part of a Nation, depending upon the level at which it is perceived and assessed. We would like to simplify and clarify our statement using an example; what is the accountability of a teacher to the nation with respect to education? A teacher must teach proficiently and make it comprehensible to his pupil, ignite eagerness in their minds, motivate and inspire them to learn more. The teacher at the same time, must keep himself abreast with latest developments in his area of specialization (irrespective of the level he is involved in teaching) to improve knowledge and in the words of Late Dr. Sarvapalli Radhakrishnan– "A teacher must himself remain a student life-long". He should inculcate a certain value system among his students and must place before them, some standards to achieve, some aims to make targets and excite eagerness in them to labour for the same. A Teachers' duty is to induce lofty ideals in his students, a sense of Nationalism and longing for his serving the humanity as a whole and recommend to his students some of good works of various intellectuals to be read.

Obviously when a teacher does not come to the class prepared or does not teach, he is not doing his job with accountability. And when a Nation spends money on education without ensuring accountability on the part of the teachers, responsible for spreading literacy and education and molding the future generations for enlightened citizenship is itself irresponsible and guilty of violating accountability to its taxpayers.

Accountability of an individual scientist

To be called a 'Scientist' is a rare privilege and demands unchallenged honesty, impartiality, objectivity and abiding faith in the soundness of his knowledge, methodology, logic and reason. What is then the accountability of a scientist? To whom he is accountable? How has this to be judged and who should be empowered to do it? We believe that experimental science is not only an intellectual pursuit but requires tremendous amount of self-control and discipline. Therefore, a scientist is first accountable to himself or herself when recording his observations on an experiment with utmost honesty. Giant airplanes carrying 800 persons on board would not have flown non-stop between continents if the concerned scientists had not recorded experimental data during development with absolute honesty as per universal natural laws. Since

"Science" is publicly or privately funded, it is inevitable that the scientists are accountable to their respective funding agencies. The private funding agencies have their own mechanism of assessing accountability of an individual or that of a group as a whole. However, public funding could be divided into the following categories;

Public institutions and accountability on their part

In India there are institutions belonging to CSIR, Council of Scientific and Industrial Research; ICAR, Indian Council of Agricultural Research; AEC, Atomic Energy Commission; ISRO, Indian Space Research Organization; ICMR, Indian Council of Medical Research and such others. Support for scientific research projects to individual scientists or institution is also made available through Government Departments; Such as DST, Department of Science and Technology; DBT, Department of Biotechnology; Department of Environment & Forest and India Meteorological Department etc.

As against accountability to the self, an individual scientist must be accountable to the public institution or the funding agency, which has given him financial support and reposed faith and confidence in his ideas, proposal, sincerity and convictions for a larger public cause. In doing so, the authorities who sanction the project from such departments also risk their prestige, honour, impartiality and judicious sagacity for the support they have extended to the project leader purely on the facts and justification presented on the project proposal paper. The scientist so supported, in-turn owes responsibility to perform to the best of his ability and not to shatter the confidence reposed in him. A major effort must therefore be in achieving the stated objectives of the project, for an innovation, concept or filling the gap in existing knowledge on the subject, not explicitly mentioned. However, accountability does not mean surrender or obligation on the part of the scientist in any way to toe the expectations of the funding agency about the possible outcome of the sanctioned project. The scientist is expected to stick to his objectivity, unbiased gradient of his research results, resist undue pressures, and maintain secrecy of his data until complete analyses is done and results interpreted in total perspective. He should also have the guts to stand by his data, analyses, interpretation and convictions and at the same time have humility and courage to accept and own mistakes if proved incorrect at any later date. And lastly, the scientist must publish his project results in the form of a book, booklet, as a documentary repository of the new knowledge he / she created.

Normally, financial support to project is released through the institute where a scientist or a group of scientists is based. It is here, much of the troubles for the Project leader arises because of inefficient release of funds to him by his own institute, improper or inefficient store purchase procedures and administrative support and several such reasons. Therefore, it is advisable to put the entire project financial grant at the disposal of the Project leader without permitting interference from any other authority. The more we learn to trust an individual, the more is his honesty and accountability invoked. It should always be borne in mind that every funding of research activity though is aimed primarily for larger public good and cause has positive and negative aspects. Even projects that developed the inter-continental ballistic missiles (ICBM) and the atom bomb as weapons of mass destruction have enabled us to penetrate space and reach to our celestial neighbors, develop excellent global communication and navigational systems and to harness unlimited store of power from inside the nucleus of atoms.

Experience of agriculture

We feel proud of achievements in agriculture so far as the quantified data on increased crop production is concerned. However, can we attribute this success to an individual scientist? Since the early 60's, or even earlier, evolving a new improved variety of all crop types has been the primary goal of agricultural research. Most other disciplines such as soil science, soil physics, irrigation, meteorology and crop physiology etc. though equally important, were treated as only supporting and peripheral. Excellent plant-genetic material and conducive; soil, physical and environmental conditions are not exclusive but mutually complementary for plant growth and economic yields. The Indian Council of Agricultural Research (ICAR) evolved a unique mechanism of evaluating the performance of various varieties of a crop coming from different institutions. This mechanism known as the 'All India Coordinated Crop Improvement Projects' extended to almost all commercially grown cereal and plantation crops have paid rich dividends. Before a variety was incorporated in the coordinated project trial from a university / institute, it was expected to have performed consistently better than the local-check varieties at the Institute / University farm itself for four to five consecutive years.

The performance of a variety was initially judged on the basis of all India average, which represented a higher level of adaptability to soil and environmental conditions in addition to productivity. The release of a variety from an institute / university brought prestige, name and even patent rights to the institution and also to the leader of the group responsible for evolving the variety, who in most cases happened to be a plant breeder. Releasing new improved plant varieties therefore, not only became important objectives in crop improvement program but also got linked with the career progress of individuals. It led to a system where there were behind the door maneuvering and machinations, understandings and compromises on the criteria for identification of such varieties. It was therefore not uncommon to note that several names of exotic varieties associated with few celebrated names, actually did not exist anywhere in the farmer's field. Obviously, people in authority were somehow bypassing the system. This has become an inevitable systemic syndrome in government-managed institutions propelled by stiff competition for survival, wild ambitions and aspirations, lack of personal discipline, integrity, intellectual honesty and bankruptcy of moral and ethical values.

Accountability of the funding agencies

Funding agencies have the responsibility to encourage research and development. Some agencies such as the Department of Science and Technology promote scientific research in general as well as in specific areas. Funding and evaluation or monitoring is accomplished through a peer review system. There could at times be exceptions in the system when scientists think it as his birthright to be funded and later refuses to even submit a report with arrogance to question competence and capability of those involved in monitoring the progress or review the project. This could be due to some outstanding achievements made in his field of specialization. However, such exceptions are rare or few. Notwithstanding such occasional aberrations, the procedure has all-important ingredients of an appropriate peer review system. If the system fails it is because of the failure of 'Peers' who either fail to rise to the level of competence, impartiality or both.

There is also an important aspect of attitude amongst scientists in India, which often, if not always, prevents operation of peer review systems. The 'peers' in their biased or myopic judgment first realize and conclude that the project itself or achievements from it are poor and hence it should be rejected or closed. No sooner this decision is taken on a project in operation there is concern expressed by some that it would be a harsh decision. Eventually some others join the chorus and at final stage an individual emerges more important than the system or science. A good 'peer' review system requires that the reviewers judiciously evaluate the merit of the proposed project or achievements in the project. Furthermore, in any given discipline / sub-discipline it is essential that at least a dozen if not a few dozen scientists of the same / equal scientific caliber are available on the subject specialty panel. The 'caliber' of these scientists must have been recognized irrespective of the positions they occupy. However, barring a few disciplines, there are not enough such people available. I personally find it nearly impossible to identify five equally good persons, nationally and internationally respected in such important fields as; plant-nutrition, soil-biology, colloid chemistry, soil-chemical kinetics, post-harvest technology, physiological genetics, plant hormones and plant cell ultra-structure in relation to plant-growth conditions etc. In the absence of sufficient number of scientists only a few are found to be repeatedly involved in several decision-making events. The funding agencies also do not want easily to include up coming scientists in their committees obsessed as they are with the halo effect. Competence, comprehension, understanding and inter-play of ideas have no relation to age, experience and accumulated knowledge of an individual. The consequence of all this being that only the Chair or Position occupied by an individual becomes identified with knowledge and wisdom in every sphere. All superlative adjectives, privileges, power and even veto to decide to go with this. No wonder, therefore, the objective of acquiring or grabbing the 'Chair' becomes important rather than acquiring knowledge, competence and excellence. **The Golden Rule for success in the olden days was; –'First Deserve and then desire' which has now been reversed to-'First Grab by any means and then justify how best you are'.** This has become the shortest route to success these days; be it an election to the fellowship of the academies or learned societies or prestigious awards given for outstanding contribution to science. Almost like a musical chair, taking turns by rotation, awards also find bartered the same way. This can be gauged from the reply given by a celebrated individual to the question of a press reporter; "Sir, What is your specific contribution for which you have been given this award?" and the reply was "Gentleman, you better ask this question to those who have given it to me".

Although I feel embarrassed and hesitant to give a personal example, I cannot help resist the temptation of stating it. When I initiated work on soil enzymes the Divisional Research and Budget Committee (DRBC) was critical of the work taking a stand that work on soil enzymes does not fall in the domain of Soil Science. However, when I look over as Head of the Division and became Chairman of DRBC the same set of people were appreciative of the work extolling it as the first of its kind in the country. Such behavior does indeed inflate ego but not without causing great harm to the spirit of science and scientific inquiry and creativity. All this has been registered only to suggest that our system is not promoting excellence and emergence of 'peer'. Therefore, a 'peer' judgment is also, sometimes questionable.

Institutional accountability

An institution has to be a place for the generation and propagation of knowledge. In addition a research institution not only has to encourage individual scientists but also group activity with appropriate impartial criteria for credit distribution. Above all, any claim from the institution should be true within the limits of experimental confirmation. This is difficult for any large institute to practice because the mechanisms for verifying data of individual / student has not been developed. This becomes more difficult in the arena of biological and agricultural sciences where results will not be always repetitive. This has to be achieved by the exemplary standards set into the system by the Director or other Senior-level scientists. Today, no individual scientist in the field of biology or agriculture can achieve commendable results without a collective group-activity and efforts. The days of individual discoveries are almost gone. The Indian society, unfortunately, is either highly individualistic or sycophancy oriented. Therefore, a real group activity wherein a leader is recognized through his work, ability to plan experiments, raise critical questions for inquiry, interpret data and effectively communicate in written or oral expression, does not develop so easily. Once results of joint effort start coming in, everyone starts falling apart on issue of sharing credit. It is a matter of national or institutional debate if this is an expression for assertion of individuality or lack of understanding of the concept of group activity for cracking scientific problem? In any case, for one reason or other, the group activity based on the need and urgency to solve problems with a sense of responsibility has not arisen. Frequent issue of Administrative orders becomes necessary or essential to forge group activity for particular tasks, rather than appeal to the inner conscious of those who should be concerned to perform voluntarily. A well-defined task may be occasionally achieved through such mechanism but not without losing on creativity and innovation. Hence it appears that institutions are capable of evolving technology but not necessarily in doing good science. The accountability of research institution, therefore, can best be evaluated by their success in technology development rather than the growth of science. We have, therefore, to decide the measure of accountability of institutions, which cannot be the same as that of an individual.

Universities versus research institutes

Universities are the centres of learning for creating new knowledge. Whereas he research institutions are the centers of technology development. This fact has somehow been ignored in our country, as State Agricultural Universities funded by individual State Governments are responsible for extension with parallel extension network of the department of agriculture. Consequently, our expectations in respect of excellence and accountability from both universities and research institute remain the same. A part of this has happened because professors / scientists in Universities have sought and obtained funds for technology development rather than the growth of science. Most, if not all, research proposals in the area of plant sciences from universities aim at application of science and technology development. For example, instead of asking funds for characterizing genes for processes and traits, and evolving suitable systems, the emphasis is on transferring genes countering biotic and abiotic stresses. Since the resource requirements for the latter are limited in universities they end up with some papers which may be even repetitions, and resulting in none or poor technology development. Internationally, there are instances where once the potential of a research is recognized for application a tie up with related business industry is found. The latter converts research observation into marketable technology / product. As an example, it was known in the seventies that Neem (Azadrichta) kernel has the property of inhibiting nitrification and improving fertilizer-nitrogen use efficiency.

However, for long this observation could not be converted into technology and fertilizer industry did not take up manufacture of this product incorporating the inhibitor. It was much later that the industry started the production with the initiative of the scientists involved in this work. In research institutions there is a hierarchal order, whether it works or not and whether one likes or not. The lack of students, limits communication between scientists and younger minds. A true educational institution allows students to raise their queries, which represent their inquisitiveness. More such questions, greater becomes the search for truth and hence the growth of science. Once teachers become involved in technology oriented or technology programs their tolerance or interaction with inquisitive questions is reduced and finally lost. And hence science suffers. In other words, whatever science could have developed in universities also does not happen. This leads to impoverishment of universities from where bright minds must emerge. To my mind the universities have to be supported for education learning and knowledge, and their accountability has to be judged by the quality of students and science generated. Unfortunately we have mixed up things in our country. We expect technology from universities and science from research Institutes. Therefore, unless we clarify our approach to education and institutional development we will be looking for alibis or explanations for our failures.

Conclusions

In the post-independence era, our leaders with some scientific temper like Jawaharlal Nehru, C. Subramainam and others were keen to see the progress of good science and science based technology development from our educational and research institutions. They were advised that establishment of large laboratories or research institutes was the best mechanism for achieving these objectives. In this process the universities, with the exception of some, or research institutions with teaching as essential component, were given the responsibility of producing graduates and post-graduates. They were not taken as important partners in growth of science. Multiplication of State Agricultural Universities to satisfy regional aspirations resulted in a meagre distribution of budget from scarce resources. In the absence of lack or inadequate financial support, deterioration in quality of teachers has resulted in the present mess. There is no point in harping on the success stories of Sir C. V.

Raman, J. C. Bose, M. N. Saha or Srinivasa Ramanujam and quality of their science. They were neither driven by the lure of technology nor were the product of any Governmental support. They were inherently very inquisitive minds and contributed through interaction with their brilliant handpicked students. This lead to creation of schools around the brilliant minds for example; Calcutta school of Prof. J. N. Mukherjee on colloid chemistry and at IARI that of Prof. S. K Sinha on stress physiology. Such schools as a group, did work comparable to anywhere in the world. However, a deathblow for creating such schools around individuals was given by the policy to recruit scientists through a written competitive examinations, where aptitude or motivation to do research was no consideration for selections to recruit scientists. A conscious effort has to be made to support universities and other institutions of higher learning to become the centers of learning and growth of science by giving them full autonomy and freedom for selecting teachers / scientists purely on the basis of merit irrespective of cast, creed, religion or region.

(*) This thematic draft paper was conceived and prepared by Late Prof. P. K. Chhonkar*, FISS, FNAAS Past President Indian Society of Soil Science, Head, Division of Soil Science and Agricultural Chemistry, I.A.R.I. and Formerly ICAR Emeritus Scientist at I.A.R.I., New Delhi, and Advisor (Agri.) International Institute of Development Management Technology, New Delhi (Website: www.aidmat.com) and supplemented, appended and edited by Dr. A. V. Moharir, Retired Professor and Head, Division of Agricultural Physics, I.A.R.I., New Delhi. This original article is therefore a tribute to the fond memory of my esteemed friend and colleague, Prof. P. K. Chhonkar, for the benefit of students and all those concerned in re-establishing the role of universities and research institutes in cultivating and nurturing talent, excellence d innovations in Science and technology.

Form of Motion of Matter: A Kaleidoscope of Physics in Life

Introduction

The subject of physics is well known to be dealing with the kind and types of energies, their conservation, manifestations, inter-conversion and interactions with matter belonging to both the animate and the inanimate world. And all activities of human beings; be it related to manufacture, trade, transport, commerce, business, management of resources, agricultural production and his personal existence are basically nothing more than the flow and conversion of energy and interactions with matter of various kinds. Therefore, whether we are aware of this fact or not, appreciate it or do not appreciate, like this reality or do not like it, consciously try to understand its meaning, reality and significance or unconsciously ignore it, the laws of physics, physical forces and energies, operate as the undercurrent behind all material creation, manifestation, activities, existence and even in destruction not only on the Earth but in the entire universe. It is therefore imperative that as an educated and enlightened citizen of a modern civilized scientific and technologically advanced world, irrespective of our physical location on the Earth, religious faith at birth, colour of the skin, kind of human race, physical conditions of living, chosen career for education and profession for livelihood, each one of us must be educated and knowledgeable about the basic laws of physics, not necessarily in details but at least in their physical significance and more particularly about the various forms of energy and their intertwine flow. All the money we exchange in whatever currency, grocery we buy, services we purchase and management of resources we practice, are in fact the price that we pay for a bundle of energy as an economic barter deal. And this realization, knowledge, understanding and education as a 'primer' must begin from childhood at home and the primary schools in general. Therefore both the parents at home and teachers in schools and colleges, at all levels and in all streams of our education (*e.g. science, technical, engineering, medical, agriculture and even social sciences and management etc.*) owe special responsibility in educating the young generations. The situation is quite analogous to the almost compulsive training, literacy and education in using computers today. Non familiarity with computers in the twenty first century has become akin to a stigma of illiteracy. So is the case with the knowledge in physics and physical forces and energies which concern us almost every moment of our healthy existence on the Earth. In fact every one of the living creature on the Earth is immersed in an ocean of energy of various kinds and respond to a multitude of them mentally, spiritually, physiologically, biochemically, physically, and mechanically. This fact is also true in case of plants, insects, microorganisms and aquatic life forms. All forms of sciences developed by human mind are therefore nothing more than attempts to systematically study the interactions of living creatures to the stimulus of various forms and kinds of energies. Therefore, it is essential that a basic minimum knowledge in physics must be delivered and made to understand by all means before individual subjects are formally taught. There is no doubt that training for logical thinking and reasoning in sincerely learning physics goes a long way beyond academics, in building a scientifically oriented, educated, thoughtful, sagacious, judicious and a genuinely open unbiased society as a long term objective for any self-respecting sovereign nation. This is also necessary and helpful in eradicating several of our age-old social prejudices and miss-beliefs, superstitions, blind faiths, sense-less gory rituals of animal and human sacrifices in the name of religion and faiths, black magic, false sense of pseudo supremacy and honour killing for its sake and such other malaise, commonly prevalent amongst all religious faiths, communities, casts and creeds and deliberately perpetuated by the vested groups and touts in the name of rituals, traditions and culture to trap gullible individuals. It is the ignorance, fear about the unknown and lack of scientific (physics) education about the invisible world that perpetuates unscientific, illogical and at times cruel practices amongst all sections of population, literates, illiterates and the unthoughtful educated-illiterates. This may be exemplified from the still prevalent practice of attributing the cause for outbreak of epidemic viral diseases such as chickenpox and smallpox to the curse of female deities (DEVIS) in India and more recently, a few years ago the magnitude of mass ignorance about science was witnessed in the mad hysterical race to temples all over the country to offer and see Lord Ganesh idols miraculously drinking milk. A properly trained and educated physicist / common man of conviction instantly perceives the interflow of energies in a given situation and in most certain cases arrives at a very logical, scientific and reasonable understanding. In short, logic, unbiased reasoning, scientific tests, experimental demonstration, critical analysis and open mind to accept new knowledge must prevail over all other stray considerations. And the best mental training in doing so is certainly received in honestly learning physics and mathematics with eagerness. A notable example demonstrating truth about such a connection can be cited here from the personal memoirs of the former President of India Dr. A.P.J. Abdul Kalam, who clearly mentions that despite the society in Rameshwaram where he lived, being highly stratified into orthodox groups, he never felt differences because of social rebels in his Science (Physics) Teacher Mr. Sivasubramaniam Iyer and some others who not only defied all prevalent norms with a candid determination to change the social system and frequently invited young Abdul Kalam over lunch and dinner to his house as a personal example for others to emulate. Human history is replete with examples where only scientists and scientifically oriented individuals have been instrumental in changing the traditional mindset of the generations and bring about radical social reforms. Incorrect, illogical and unreasonable and unscientific practices of any kind (religious, cult, faith or tradition etc.) on whatever pretext, if once allowed to gain ground and perpetuate in society, it would take centuries and even millennium to get rid of their nuisance and malaise. Werner Heisenberg, the celebrated physicist and inventor of 'Quantum Mechanics' has also said that the greatest effort is always necessary at those points where one has to abandon old concepts. The eradication of the 'Sati-Pratha' self or forced immolation of the wife of a deceased husband is an example of this kind. The recent spurt in the incidences of 'honour killings' for various reasons being reported in the media these days is another social malaise of this kind that needs to be dealt with heavy hand. And reasons for all such gory practices are surely the lack of modern scientific education, mind set and un-reasonable blind-faith. There is therefore no substitute to rigorously spreading, promoting, encouraging, learning and teaching of physics and related physical sciences for building an objective, rational, judicious and progressive society. It is unfortunate, that our Scientific and Academic bodies (like

ICMR) should not be in a position to initiate studies on such subjects as 'Family *Gotras*' traditionally inherited and held close to the hearts by people in almost all states in the country to look into the scientific basis, their relation (if any) to the human blood groups, genetic basis and significance for marriages of individuals born within and between different '*Gotras*" and continued relevance in the twenty-first century. Ten or twenty Ph. D. level student fellowships regularly given on All India basis for a period of ten years would at least scientifically see this problem in proper perspective or even resolve the problem for ever. This is particularly urgent in view of sporadic violence, murders and crimes being done and innocent lives are cruelly terminated. India has resolved earlier a contentious issue of 52 different calendar systems prevalent in the country and being religiously adhered to by various communities, in evolving a National Calendar through consensus. A similar approach after doing a thorough scientific research needs to be adopted for the problem of '*Gotras*' and various other orthodox problems that plague the social cause and lives in this country. It would be ridiculous to leave them just as such to the prevalent blind faith or social beliefs and not attempting to find or prove a scientific basis in them. I am sure, I am liable to be questioned- How learning physics and social problems described above have anything in common? And with all sincerity and conviction, I admit that there is not only connection but all our problems originate from non-compliance and non-subordination to the natural laws that govern our very existence on the Earth.

How physics is integral to education and life

Under the present scenario, lessons in physics and mathematics should be made mandatory for the students of all biological sciences and particularly in agricultural sciences because they are directly and primarily concerned with the use of natural solar energy in terms of photosynthesis and the yields of plant and agricultural produce. All the efforts, indulged into, by the agricultural scientists in breeding and hybridization of new crop plant varieties for increased or optimized yields are, in fact directed towards efficient harnessing and utilization of solar energy under normal or specific environmental conditions from various locations. A critical scientific look at the crop breeding programs pursued by the agricultural plant breeders will reveal that the measures adopted by them are indeed directed to bringing about necessary changes in the existing varieties in terms of increased biomass production, qualitative and quantitative changes in protein, carbohydrate and sugar syntheses and other associated changes besides appealing colour, shape and size, taste, cooking qualities, economic production, resistance to pests and diseases, partitioning of harnessed solar energy for auto-synthesis of insect toxins (Bt.) for self-protection by the crop plants and for enhanced post-harvest shelf life. And all these involve complex dynamics of energy harnessing, transportation, biosynthesis and storage of molecules within plant cells to produce what we call the crop yield. Such changes are mediated through changes incorporated into the DNA sequence of the concerned crop plant-cell using several well-known conventional and modern molecular genetics techniques for gene transfer. Complexities arise because most of the characters of crop plants are controlled by multiple genes and their sequential locations on the DNA molecular strand. Understanding of the energy basis of nature and of the physical processes that are involved for maximizing energy harnessing in any of the physical, physiological, biochemical, metabolic and biosynthetic processes is therefore essential to modulate, regulate and engineer crop plants suitable for new requirements and demands. No wonder, crop plant breeding is not an isolated enterprise but an activity that needs considerable inputs from physics and physical sciences (Meteorology, Soil Physics, and Agronomy that is intimately related to micrometeorology and various kinds of 'morphogenetic energy fields'). And such conscious integration of different disciplines was one of the main reasons indeed for the success of the All India Coordinated Crop Improvement Projects launched by the Indian Council of Agricultural Research (ICAR) in the early sixties that led to the first green revolution.

Reasons for location specificity of crop plant species and varieties

Rupert Sheldrake, the well-known biologist has recently come out with his path breaking 'New Science of Life' the role of physical forces and morphogenetic fields in what is called the morphogenesis of organic molecules and forms within living organisms. Several reports of studies conducted by the NASA-USA also corroborate the fact that radiations, electrically charged plasma, coronal mass ejections, solar flares etc from the Sun and outer galaxy affect the geo-magnetic fields on the Earth and life forms in both positive and negative ways. And it is time; investigations on the components of such morphogenetic fields are intensified. Perhaps, Physics departments in agricultural research institutions can take a lead. There appears great potential in this area of research as much of the problems of photosensitivity and location specificity in some cash crops such as cotton, *durum* and *dicoccum* wheat, spices from tropical humid climatic locations, alfonso mangoes from Ratnagiri, citrus and oranges from Vidarbha region of Maharashtra, coconut plantations along sea coastal regions etc. and the crypto-biological aspects of insect-pest proliferation despite huge loads of insecticide and pesticide applications over the years, can be possibly linked to the presence or absence of strong or weak morphogenetic fields at various locations. Recently, Hugh Lovel an organic and biodynamic pioneer, who developed a device called 'Quantum Field Broadcaster' combining principles of quantum physics, biochemistry and the mind / body link, demonstrated the use of his stationary self-driven devise that induces self-reinforcing, resonant fractal patterns, like homeopathic potencies, directly into the life energy fields of soil and atmosphere. It not only improves the patterns of lime in the soil related to mineral release, nitrogen fixation, digestion and providing nutrients to plants, it also works with the atmospheric patterns of silica related to photosynthesis, blossoming, fruiting and ripening. Healthy lime and silica patterns are also believed to have the potential to change rainfall patterns and restore health to barren lands. Another classic and yet baffling example of how possibly, morphic / morphogenetic fields modified by the presence of soluble and other impurities in water from any location on the earth affect the shape, size, symmetry and purity of snow, ice and water crystals formed from that water has been clearly demonstrated by a Japanese practioner of Alternative Medicines Dr. Masaru Emoto. And such snow and water crystals have also been reported to be responding to mental energies and human emotions through possibly morphic resonance (my interpretation). This seems logical because water constitutes over 90% of human, insect, animal and plant body masses.

This paper advocates the need for reorienting and strengthening teaching of physics in schools, colleges, engineering, medical and agricultural universities and in management oriented academic institutions for overall comprehension of the complex problems in a holistic way and more than this; to empower our young graduates and post graduates in tackling challenging problems of enhanced food production and food security for the billions living on the earth or mass-production of consumer goods for human comfort and necessities. Physics is not merely a 'subject for study' for a university degree but a 'religion by itself' and a philosophy for life and our existence on the Earth. Because the only Universal Religion for every one of us is to collectively and individually maintain himself / herself mentally, thoughtfully, physiologically, nutritionally and physically in sound good health, depending upon geographical location on the earth, because food intake, its nature and effective digestion by the body's metabolism are mediated to a great extent by the external environmental conditions and mental strategies to combat them for survival. This is the only meaning of spirituality and essence of all religions, past or present that have flourished on earth. Almost all the so erroneously called 'religious texts' of ancient Indian history e.g.; Vedas, Upanishads and Geeta are indeed scientific treatises. It is our negligence in learning the Sanskrit language that has alienated us from the science (as modern as we can think of) contained in them. Late Dr. M.R. Guney, a Nuclear Physicist from the Bhabha Atomic Research Centre has clearly brought out the scientific aspect of the Geeta in his book in Marathi-'Dnyaneshwari che Bhava-vishwa' *(The Emotional World of Dnyaneshwari – a treatise on Geeta in Marathi written by Sant Dnyaneshwar over 700 years ago).*

Form of motion of matter

The Concept of "Basic Forms of Motion" embraces an extremely wide domain of phenomena into which the whole of nature can be broken down and to which, all natural sciences including all processes constituting the structural elements and interactions taking place in them are included.

Form of motion is;

1. Associated with a definite type of matter,
2. Have qualitative features of a certain family of phenomena or motions distinguishing it from other such family,
3. Related to internal structure of the material entity,
4. Related to the type of interaction between the elements constituting the given entity and its structure,

Interrelation of traditionally classified sciences, reflect the interrelation of forms of motion, and consequently the forms of energies, extending to the basic fundamental concepts of each science. For Physics, this fundamental concept is "Nature, Kind and Form of Energy" for Chemistry it is "Chemical Element" for Biology, the concept of "Species" or may be "DNA / RNA". Any quantitative research based on mathematical logic not only changes the quality but even the scales of accuracy for a meaningful comprehension of the phenomena / problem under investigation, its practical utility and for evolving or converting the results into practical technologies. Physics provides the necessary theoretical and experimental approach and mathematics, the necessary logic for quantitative measurements. Several examples of the intertwining of the conclusions of different sciences can be seen, not only in the development of the sciences called geology, geochemistry, geophysics, cosmology and astronomy but even in the biological sciences such as genetics, biophysics, biochemistry, physiology, molecular biology / genetics and biotechnology. For example, to study the upper part of the earth's crust, cooperation between ancient geology, geophysics and geochemistry has been established. But, to probe the deeper layers of the crust, specially the mantle and the core, geological methods prove ineffective and physics, astrophysics / stellar physics, astronomy, geophysics and geochemistry come to the fore. Geophysics provides information on density, elasticity, viscosity, electrical and magnetic properties, heat flow from the interior to the earth's surface and information regarding thermal history of the earth in general. Physics provides theoretical and experimental data regarding the properties of matter at high pressures and temperatures to validate geophysical conclusions. Whereas, astronomy, astrophysics provides information concerning the distribution of mass within the earth, mechanical properties of the globe as a whole, its gravitational field, changes in the latitudes due to the shifting of the magnetic poles and fluctuations in the spatial orientation of the earth's axis of rotation and cosmogony theories about the origin of the earth, the solar system and individual planets of the solar system. The interactions, mutual understanding and appreciation between specialists working in narrow areas of their individual specialty grows on the strength of increased use of quantitative analysis, analytical tools and holistic approaches from multidisciplinary angles.

It is known and well established that chemical, physical, mechanical and biological processes taking place on the earth have contributed to the evolution of a large number of transitory boundary sciences. The totality of all such sciences can be represented in the following table;

Astromechanics	Geomechanics	Biomechanics
Astrophysics	Geophysics	Biophysics
Astrochemistry	Geochemistry	Biochemistry

The two other transitional sciences between physics and chemistry include 'physical chemistry' and 'chemical physics'.

The **horizontal rows** and **vertical columns** in the above table exhibit the **deepest** and the most **intrinsic** relationship links respectively amongst themselves. However, in considering the interrelation of sciences, it should be borne in mind that each science has its specific method of research, tools, theories and relationship with each other, their subject matter, its common origin and scale and magnitude of the forces and energies involved. Therefore, overall comprehension can never be achieved without the broadest utilization of the knowledge of physics, chemistry, mathematics and modern engineering and it would be futile to expect worthwhile contribution without inputs from these disciplines and knowledge about the interactions of matter with various form and kinds of energies.

Experiments conducted in changing the conventionally traditional sequence in the order of teaching biology-chemistry-physics in schools to physics—chemistry and then biology, has led to a significant logical flow of conceptual understanding amongst students from physics to chemistry to biology, better mathematical reinforcement, increased appreciation and enrollment of students to physics courses, enhanced curiosity and scientific literacy besides compulsive urge to understand physical sciences. As biology and agriculture continue to become more and more sophisticated and knowledge intensive subjects with the wide scale use and applications of such physical tools as X-Ray diffractometer, transmission and scanning electron microscopes, scanning tunneling electron microscope and atomic force microscope, confocal microscope, nuclear magnetic resonance spectroscopes, nuclear techniques, mass spectrometer, chromatography techniques, electrophoreses, computers, computing technologies, information theories and technology, mathematical and computer modeling, statistical theories and satellite borne and ground based remote sensing, there is a growing demand for human resource equipped with knowledge and comprehension of physics, mathematics and chemistry for not only better understanding the concepts in biological sciences, but for their applications. The important role of physics and physical laws as the under-current of all agricultural activities from sowing and germination of seeds to the harvest, storage, appropriate packing material, transportation, distribution and hygienically safe disposal still continue to be ignored, unsolicited and seldom appreciated in full measure, despite several serious instances of sporadic and epidemic spread of crop diseases, insect-pest infestations arising out of unsafe storage and distribution of agricultural produce in public for human consumption. The role of physical conditions and environment for prolific growth of pathogenic micro flora over agricultural produce during storage and transportation is very much appreciated but never practically enforced in all seriousness as mandatory regulatory conditions.

Very few of our mushrooming 'Central and State Agricultural Universities' have established strong groups or programs in teaching and research in physics and physical sciences in relation to the requirements and demands of hygienic storage, processing, packaging, sanitization, transportation and distribution of our innumerable agricultural, horticultural, floricultural and even forest-related products. The present complacent situation needs to be changed at the earliest. The emphasis should be on generation of knowledge in a holistic way rather than setting boundaries limited to disciplines or sub-disciplines. All existing agricultural universities and other agricultural research institutions in the country must evolve a mechanism to work out problems in a multi-disciplinary action plan. This would not only end the isolation of our exclusively established 'Agricultural University' system from basic scientific disciplines but help in raising standards of teaching, research, education, human resource and technology development.

Challenging job opportunities can be created for physicists, willing to make career in the field of agriculture, where their knowledge can be gainfully employed to advantage. These include areas of growing crops under low input conditions of water, fertilizers and chemicals, high and low altitude and gravity conditions including space, agricultural meteorology, defining conditions of crop production under fluctuating climatic and global warming scenario, food processing, preservation, storage and technology, precision agriculture, grade and quality evaluation of agricultural produce, quality certification, molecular genomics, bio-molecular identification, isolation, purification, characterization, structure determination, preservation, storage and search for applications in other areas. All these may require readjustments / reorientation of certain existing sections under related disciplines and faculties for focused priorities.

Any talk of intellectual property right protection, preservation and conservation of crop, insect, forest flora and fauna, aquatic and marine biodiversity and such related issues without physical, genetic and bio-molecular characterization will receive little or no consideration and credibility. We need to establish strong schools and create infrastructure for education and training of human resource for jobs in these prime areas that require greater understanding of physics, physical laws, their limits, range and mode of operation on a war footing. In fact, time is running out and in the event of further neglect, a disaster unimaginable may befall. All these activities demand induction and recruitment of individuals who are capable, eager and willing to excel and perform with utmost honesty and sincerity. Quality science and related services can certainly be achieved through open competition and not through restrictive reserved pastures. There is still time for our exclusive agricultural universities to rectify the situation. It must be realized that all the best known institutes of technology and engineering in the world are also very strong centers of teaching, training, research and developments in physics, chemistry, mathematics and biological sciences. Recent developments in our Indian Institutes of Technology embarking on introducing medical, and medical technology courses is a step in the right direction. If agriculture essentially constitutes a holistic technology for optimizing and maximizing crop productivity, there is full justification to strengthen strong teaching, training and research programs in basic disciplines in agricultural universities. Without them, I am afraid; there may be little hope for any meaningful significant contribution coming forth.

References for further reading

1. Rupert Sheldrake, 'The Hypothesis of a New Science of Life-Morphic Resonance'; Park Street Press, 1995.

2. 'The Interaction of Sciences in The Study of the Earth' Translated from originally in Russian By Vladimir Talmy (Editorial Board: V.I. Baranov, Y.V. Karus, I.V. Kuznetsov, D.I. Shcherbakov, V.V. Tikhomirov and Y.P. Trusov). Progress Publishers, Moscow, 1968.

3. Segre, Gino. 'Einstein's Refrigerator-Tales of the hot and cold', Allen Lane-An imprint of Penguine Books, 2002.

4. Segre, Gino, 'A Matter of Degrees-What temperature reveals about the past and future of our species, planet, and universe'. Penguine Books, 2003.

5. Foster Russell and Leon Kreitzman, 'Seasons of Life-The biological rhythms that living things need to thrive and survive', Profile Books, 2009.

6. Ho, Mae-Wan, 'The Rainbow and the Worm-The Physics of Organisms', World Scientific, 2008.

7. Cowan, David and Anne Silk, 'Ancient Energies of the Earth. A ground breaking exploration of the Earth's natural energy and how it affects our health'. Thorsons- An Imprint of Harper Collins Publishers, 1999.

8. Abdul Kalam, A.PJ, with Arun Tiwari, 'Wings of Fire- An Autobiography', Universities Press, Hyderabad, 1999.

9. Becker, R.O. and Gary Selden, 'The Body Electric-Electromagnetism and the Foundation of Life', Harper, 1985.

10. Bentlet, W.A. and W.J. Humphreys; Snow Crystals (Dover, 1962) The original Book was published by McGraw Hill in 1931.

11. Nakaya, U. Snow Crystals: Natural and Artificial, Harvard University Press, 1954.

12. Emoto Masaru, The Hidden Messages in Water, Translated from the original in Japanese by David A Thayne, ATRIA Books, 2001.

13. Guney, M.R., Dnyaneshwari che Bhava Vishwa, In Marathi, 2006, Snehal Prakashan, Pune, India, pp 192.

14. Lovel Hugh, Quantum Agriculture, P.O. Box 898, Tolga, Queensland 4882. Telephone 61-495 567.

Dr. Anil Vishnu Moharir

(b: February 04, 1944 at Nagpur, Maharashtra, India)

Summary Statement on the Contribution of Dr. Anil Vishnu Moharir to Science

Anil Vishnu Moharir, holds B.Sc. 1965 (Physics, Chemistry, Mathematics) and M.Sc. 1967 (Physics) degrees from the Jiwaji University Gwalior and Ph.D. 1980 degree from the Indian Institute of Technology-Delhi. He started his scientific research career from the National Physical Laboratory in 1967 and was engaged in the project for preparing Selenium photoconductive cells under the guidance of Dr. V. G. Bhide, then Deputy Director, NPL. He joined the Indian Council of Agricultural Research (ICAR) Service in December 1968 and served in various capacities as Senior Research Assistant, Scientist, Principal Scientist, Professor and Head, Division of Agricultural Physics. He worked on spectroscopic, spectro-photometric and electron microscopic studies of soils, plants and other biological materials and developed accurate spectro-photometric methods for trace determination of Iron and Titanium, which have now been listed in text books of analytical chemistry. As a practicing electron microscopy specialist, he developed many innovative, sample processing techniques for practical transmission electron microscopy of biological materials and developed a new procedure - 'Contact Electron Micrography' for characterization of paper and thin film materials. Based on his studies on 'Moisture Hysteresis Curves of Seeds of Cereal Crops', he developed a simple laboratory procedure for screening drought tolerant wheat and rice varieties for cultivation under rain-fed conditions and introduced a new concept of 'Normalized-Moisture-Hysteresis' for comparative evaluation of genotypes, which has found practical use in bakery and biscuit industry in increasing the shelf life of bakery products by DANONE Biscuits, Belgium.

Later, he studied the fine structure and structure-property relationships in native cotton fibres of all the four commercially cultivated species *(Gossypium- herbaceum, Gossypium arboretum, Gossypium hirsutm and Gossypium barbadense)* for helping cotton breeders in selecting parent genotypes for evolving new strains with inherent high fibre tenacity through genetic hybridization as demanded by the modern high speed cotton processing and Open-End Spinning (OES Or Rotor Spinning) technology. From X-Ray diffraction studies on cotton fibres, he identified Hermans Cellulose Crystallite Orientation Index to be the best parameter for characterization of cotton for tensile strength of fibres, within individual *diploid* and *tetraploid* species and within a mixture of all species taken together. He has published over one hundred thirty research papers in national and international journals, presented several at conferences held in India, Germany, Belgium and USA as an invited 'Keynote Speaker'. He has translated and edited several books, poems, religious texts from Hindi and Marathi into English and served as Honorary Editor of the Indian Journal of Fibre and Textile Research (CSIR), New Delhi, Journal of Agricultural Research Karnal, Haryana, India, Chief Editor of the Journal of Agricultural Physics, New Delhi, and a regular referee for other scientific journals and as a Panel Scientist for the e-Text Book project of the National Institute of Science Communication (NISCOM-CSIR) New Delhi.

A recipient of prestigious fellowships from the IAEA, Vienna and the Commission of the European Communities, Brussels, Prof. Moharir has handled two international collaborative research projects on structure-property relationship in native cotton. He has travelled in England, Europe, Russia (USSR) and USA. Over half a dozen biographical compilations have listed him, consecutively for over a decade for his contribution to science. Interested in Hindustani classical music, Prof. Moharir is himself an accomplished portrait artist in charcoal medium. In New Delhi, he had been actively associated with various social, educational and cultural organizations and served the prominent the Maratha Mitra Mandal in various capacities as member of the Executive Committee, Joint Secretary and Secretary for over twenty long years under presidentship of Late Shri Annasaheb (A.P.) Shinde and Shri Shankarrao B. Chavan.

After retirement in 2006, he is regularly writing freelance on scientific subjects from multi-disciplinary angles. His book- 'Profile in Solitude-Felicitation of Professor Atmaram Bhairav (A. B.) Joshi on his Ninety first Birthday' with Foreword from Professor M. S. Swaminathan, FRS, FNA, is a *de-facto* national document on the life and contribution of Dr. Atmaram Bhairav (A. B.) Joshi, to the first Green Revolution. His other books- 'A Life of a Physicist in Agricultural Research' and 'Random Walks in Solitude-Essays in Multidisciplinary Explorations in Science' are unique and scholarly contributions to science. His books –'A Scientific Look at the Concept of Soul: An Attempted Synthesis', Zorba Books, Gurugram, India 2017 and 'A Scientific Look at the Concepts of Soul, Rebirth, Work and the Law of Karma: An Attempted Synthesis' Zorba Books, Second Revised and enlarged edition 2019 are the scholarly, innovative, multidisciplinary interpretations, based on modern science, of the ancient concepts of Soul, Rebirth, Work and the Law of Karma.

Professor Moharir served as a member of the National Panel of Eminent Citizens, Ministry of Rural Development, Government of India, for evaluation of the projects executed under the Mahatma Gandhi National Rural Employment Guarantee Scheme (MGNREGA) in the state of Nagaland for over two years.

After living and serving for 76 years in New Delhi, Dr Moharir has shifted to Pune, Maharashtra with his family since February 2021.